G000141796

From Caesar to the Sax

The story of Roman Britain
Graham Tingay M.A.

Head of the Classics Department,
King's College School, Wimbledon

Longman

LONGMAN GROUP LIMITED
London

*Associated companies, branches and representatives
throughout the world*

First published 1969
New impression 1977

ISBN 0 582 31359 7

*Printed in Hong Kong by
Sing Cheong Printing Co Ltd*

We are grateful to the following for permission to reproduce copyright
material: The British Printing Corporation Limited for an extract from
Roman Silchester by G. C. Boon; J. M. Dent and Sons Ltd and E. P. Dutton
and Co. Inc. for an extract from *Caesar's War Commentaries* edited and translated by John Warrington, Everyman Library Edition, and Dutton Paper-
back Edition (1958) respectively.

Preface

We live in what was the Roman province of Britannia, and it is only natural that we should want to find out about a fascinating period of our country's history. Moreover, we could hardly have a better introduction to the working of the Roman empire and the wealth of its civilisation. The new syllabuses for O-level and C.S.E. Latin, devised by various examining boards, now offer the chance to study the Romans in Britain, encouraging us to turn directly to the words, whether in the original or translation, of ancient writers. The accounts in Greek and Latin that have come down to us are impressive and varied: the material evidence in Britain may be slight in comparison with the remains in other provinces, but our archaeologists' skill in extracting information from it is unparalleled.

It is difficult, and often impossible for students in schools, to get at all this evidence: accordingly I have tried to write a simple account of Roman Britain, with direct quotation of the literary sources, inscriptions and archaeological evidence where this is possible. But its history is not simple and clear-cut. There is no certain answer to many problems, yet I thought it more suitable in a book of this nature to choose from what seemed to me the best opinions I could find, and to omit the 'perhaps' or 'probably' which ought to qualify so many statements.

It is also impossible in this book to attribute to their authors the opinions and examples I have used, even if I could do so. I am greatly in the debt of the authors listed in Chapter 23, and can only hope that they will consider the mention of them there to be some measure of adequate acknowledgement.

The translations of the passages of Caesar come from *Caesar's War Commentaries* by J. Warrington, except for his description of Britain and its people: this, and all the other translations are by me. I have above all tried to make their meaning clear to school students, accepting the loss of other qualities this has entailed.

I am deeply grateful to Miss Norma Miller, of Royal Holloway College, to David E. Johnston, Staff Tutor in Archaeology, Southampton University, and to a former pupil, R. J. A. Wilson, who have read the typescript and saved me from many errors; those that remain are entirely due to my own obstinacy and ignorance.

Contents

The Mildenhall dish

1

First Contacts

Throughout the afternoon and into the evening of August 25th, 55 BC, nearly ten thousand men had been mustering on the beaches of Boulogne, and systematically embarking in the eighty transports drawn up in the surf. A little before midnight, with a fair wind from the south, they cast off and sailed for the shores of Kent. For the first time Roman legions were to land on this island, which was to become, in time, a small but not unimportant part of a huge and powerful empire. Their commander was Caius Julius Caesar. Of all the invaders who have come to our country only he has left his own account of what he did.

'Summer was now drawing to a close, and winter sets in rather early in those parts, as Gaul lies wholly in northern latitudes. Nevertheless, I hurried on preparations for an expedition to Britain, knowing that Britain had rendered assistance to the enemy in nearly all my Gallic campaigns. Although it was too late in the year for military operations I thought it would be a great advantage merely to have visited the island, to have seen what kind of people the inhabitants were, and to have learned something about the country with its harbours and landing-places. Of all this the Gauls knew virtually nothing; for no one except traders makes the journey with any regularity, and even their knowledge is limited to the sea coast immediately facing Gaul. Interviews with numerous merchants elicited nothing as to the size of the island, the names and strength of the native tribes, their military and civil organization, or the harbours which might accommodate a large fleet. Nevertheless it seemed essential to obtain this information before risking an expedition, and Caius Volusenus appeared to me the best man for the job. He travelled in a warship with orders to make a general reconnaissance and report back as early as possible.'

We shall see later that the men interviewed by Caesar must have been lying, for they could have told him nearly everything he wanted to know. But Caesar might well have done some research himself: he could speak Greek fluently, and several Greeks had written of the 'Bretannic isles'; a little of what they wrote has survived till today.

The very first mention of Britain occurs in a book by the historian Herodotus. He tells the story of the great wars fought between the Greeks and

The world according to Herodotus

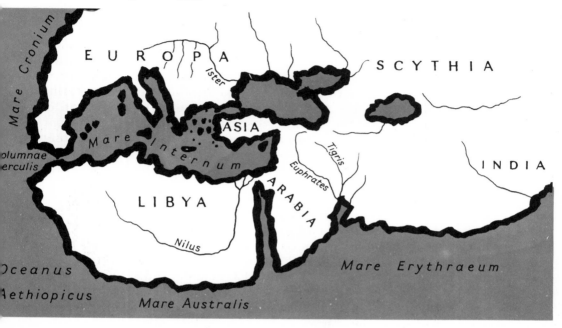

Persians in the first twenty years of the fifth century BC, and there is a fascinating series of digressions about the different countries he visited: the map represents his idea of what the world looked like.

'But,' he says, 'I do not know the islands called the Cassiterides, from which our tin comes.'

The Greek word for tin is *kassiteros*, which comes from Sanskrit, an old Indian language, and tin is found in the islands on the coast of India. It is assumed that the Phoenicians first brought the name from the East together with the metal, and that in the course of their trading cruises they took the name with them to Cornwall and the Scilly Isles. There is a *Cassiter Street* in Bodmin. Herodotus died in 430 BC.

Roughly a hundred years later Pytheas, a navigator from the Greek colony at Marseilles, sailed round the 'Northern Seas', and put Britain firmly on the map. His own words have not survived, but other ancient writers often quote him, even though they believed that most of his reports were the 'tall stories' that sailors love to tell. He sailed from Cadiz, past Gibraltar, north by Ushant to Cornwall and St. Michael's Mount, where there was a tin trading post; he then sailed right round Britain, describing its inhabitants and weather. He tells us that the tribes were independent, ruled by kings, and preserved their ancient customs: they used chariots in war, for instance, just like the Greek heroes in the Trojan War. Their dwellings were humble, made of logs and thatch; they stored their grain crops in covered pits or barns, and brewed a drink from corn and honey.

Model of an Iron-age chariot, drawn by two small horses

A reconstruction of the farm at Little Woodbury

A farmstead belonging to this period, excavated at Little Woodbury, near Salisbury, in 1938, confirms Pytheas's statements. The picture shows a modern reconstruction of this three-acre site. The corn was parched and stored in pits, lined and sealed with clay to keep out the damp; when a pit became sour or mouldy it was filled with rubbish, and a new pit was dug. Corn for seed, which could not be parched, was kept in small square granaries raised on posts to keep out damp and mice.

The corn was ground in querns – portable corn-grinding mills. The bones of sheep and oxen, pigs, horses and dogs which were found indicate that the farmers kept cattle, and hunted. Fragments of spindlewhorls, and loom-weights, prove that cloth was woven; similar fragments, even pieces of cloth, from other excavations show that this skill was widespread.

A primitive corn-grinding mill, called a quern, from Worthing, Sussex

Iron-age weaving equipment from Somerset

Woven fragments found at Amesbury, near Stonehenge

11

Pytheas knew much about the tin trade.

'The inhabitants of Britain who live in Cornwall,' he said, 'are especially friendly to strangers, and from meeting foreign traders have adopted civilized habits. It is these people who produce the tin, cleverly working the land which bears it . . . they dig out the ore, melt it and purify it. Then they hammer the metal into ingots like knuckle-bones, and transport them to an island off the coast called Ictis (St. Michael's Mount), for the channel dries out at low tide, and they can take the tin over in large quantities on their carts. Merchants purchase the tin from the natives there, and ship it back to Gaul.'

From Britain he sailed on to an island called Thule, which the ancients thought was the most northerly inhabited land in the world, 'a six days' sail north of Britain, near the frozen sea.' This may have been Norway or Iceland. Perhaps the oddest of his yarns is this; it is retold by a Greek geographer called Strabo, a contemporary of Caesar.

'Pytheas, after alleging that he travelled along the whole of Britain that he could reach, reported that the total coastline was about 5,000 miles long; then he added his story about Thule, and those regions where there was no proper land or sea or air, but a sort of substance made up of all these, rather like a jellyfish, in which he says the earth, the sea and everything else is floating, and on which one can neither walk nor sail.'

These reports were written before Caesar went to Britain. Although they are vague and inaccurate, he may have read them and all the others he could find. But there cannot have been very much evidence for him; an Alexandrian named Appian, who became a high civil servant in the Roman empire, wrote, about AD 120:

'Caesar was the first Roman to cross the Rhine. He also went to Britain, an island larger than a continent (!) and *still unknown to the Romans*.'

Whatever he knew of Britain, Caesar continued his preparations.

Gaul and Britain

'Meanwhile I moved the whole army into Artois, where the mainland is nearest to the coast of Britain: and ships were ordered to assemble there from all the neighbouring districts, including the fleet which had been built last year for the Venetian campaign. However, some traders revealed our plans to the Britons, and a number of tribes sent envoys promising hostages, and offering to submit. They were received in audience, promised generous terms, and urged to abide by their undertaking. They were accompanied on their return journey by Commius, whom I had appointed ruler of the Atrebates after the conquest of that tribe, and of whose honour, discretion and loyalty I had received abundant proof. Commius was greatly respected in Britain, and his orders were to visit all the states he could, impressing on them the advantages of Roman protection, and to announce my impending arrival. Volusenus completed his survey as far as he was able without disembarking and risking a hostile reception from the natives. Five days later he returned and made his report.'

Later in his book Caesar describes these natives, and the country they lived in.

'The central regions of Britain are inhabited by a people who claim, relying on their folk-lore, to have originated there; on the coast live the immigrant Belgae, who came to plunder and fight, but stayed to cultivate the land. Nearly all these have kept the names of the states from which they came. The population is very large; they have many houses, rather like those in Gaul, and large herds. They use bronze or gold coins, or, as an alternative, iron rods of fixed weight. Tin is found inland, and small quantities of iron near the coasts, but they import their copper. Apart from the beech and fir, there are trees of every kind as in Gaul. They think it is wrong to eat hares or chickens or geese, but they breed them as pets. As the cold is less severe, the climate is more temperate than in Gaul.
'The island is triangular, and one side, about 475 miles long, is opposite Gaul. Kent forms one corner, and nearly all the ships from Gaul land there. This side points east, while the other end points south. Another side looks west towards Spain; the Britons reckon it is roughly 665 miles long. In this direction is Ireland, which they believe is about half the size of Britain, and about the same distance away from it as Gaul. In the middle of the Irish Channel is the Isle of Man; they think there are a number of smaller islands off the coast. Some geographers have written that in midwinter, in these islands, there are thirty days' continual darkness. Though I made enquiries, I could find nothing about this, but we did discover from accurate measurement by water-clock that the nights are shorter than on the continent. The third side, thought to be 760 miles long, looks north, with no land opposite, but one corner points roughly towards Germany. The circumference of the whole island measures 1,900 miles.
'The most civilised people are those in Kent, which is entirely a coastal area; they have much the same customs as the Gauls. Most of those living further inland do not sow corn, but live on milk and flesh, and wear clothes made of animal skins. All the Britons, though, dye their skin with woad, which produces a blue colour, and thereby look all the more terrifying in battle. They do not cut their hair, but shave all the rest of the body except the head and upper lip.

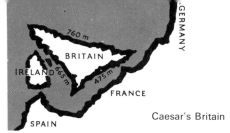
Caesar's Britain

Wives are shared between groups of ten or twelve men, usually made up of brothers, or fathers and sons. The children are reckoned as belonging to the man each girl marries first.'

This account contains many mistakes: much of the information about the metal mines is wrong; corn was grown, cloth was woven. Let us compare with it another description of the island and its people written by the geographer Strabo a few years after the death of Caesar. Strabo again tells us that the island is triangular, and explains its position with regard to Gaul; he adds some information:

'There are four routes normally used for crossing from the continent, each beginning from the mouth of a river, the Rhine, the Seine, the Loire and the Garonne. However, those who set out from the Rhine area do not sail from the river itself, but from the land of the Morini, where Boulogne is, the naval base used by the deified Caesar . . . Most of the island is level and well-wooded, but there are many hilly districts. It produces corn, cattle, gold, silver and iron. These are all exported, together with leather, slaves and good hunting-dogs. The Gauls use these dogs, and their own, for war, as well.

'The men of Britain are taller than the Gauls, but less compact; their hair is darker, too. To give an indication of their size, I myself saw some of their youngsters in Rome, at least half a head taller than the tallest Romans, though they were bandy-legged and gawky.'

He adds a few remarks about Ireland, though he admits he has no reliable witnesses for his statements:

'I have nothing very certain to say about this island, except that its inhabitants are less civilised than the British, for they eat great quantities of food – and men as well. Moreover they consider it an honourable thing, when their fathers die, to eat them . . .'

So much, for the moment, for the accounts of ancient writers. It is from archaeological evidence that we can draw different, often more accurate, pictures of what the people and land were like when Caesar arrived.

Digging up History

We can learn some of the history of Roman Britain from the books of ancient writers, and some from the study of what we can see on the earth's surface, or is revealed by careful excavation. We need both sources of knowledge: one is not enough without the other. For example, ancient writers speak of various walls built across the north of England by the emperors Hadrian, Antoninus and Severus; Gildas, a Welsh Christian priest, who wrote about AD 540, believed that such walls were only built at the very end of Roman rule. Until the middle of last century it was commonly thought that what we know as Hadrian's Wall was built by the emperor Severus, who died in York in AD 211. But inscriptions found since then have made it clear that the Wall was built by Hadrian's general Platorius Nepos, after the emperor had personally inspected the region in AD 122, and that Severus had it rebuilt eighty years later.

Though it is highly unlikely that any more literary evidence for Roman Britain will be found, archaeologists are constantly unearthing more material remains and, better still, learning to interpret the meaning of these things more accurately.

Stonehenge

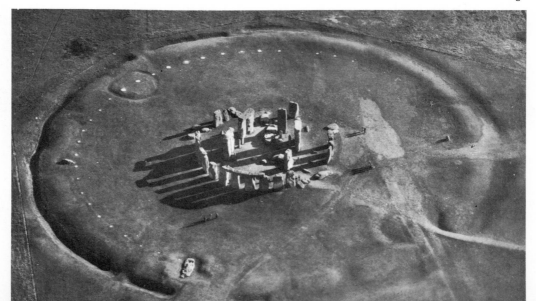

Maiden Castle, in Dorset

Some remains are very easy to find. The earth ramparts of the many Iron-Age hill-forts in the West Country rise high above the fields, and great stone circles like Stonehenge are not uncommon. Hadrian's Wall marches

The walls of the Roman fort at Richborough, Kent

over the fells, while the stone villages and brochs of north Scotland and the Orkneys still wait patiently for their visitors. In nearly every county we can walk over the roads the Romans built; the walls of their forts even now rise above our heads, while we can still stumble into the quarries from which they cut their stone, or peer into the mines which gave them lead and copper, even gold.

From the foundations and rubble of great houses and small farms, now often lying many feet below the surface of the soil, have come coins and tools, and thousands of pieces of pots and jugs. In the graves of ancient warriors or kings, their children or their slaves, we find jewels, toys and, of course, their ashes or their bones. And most important of all in our attempt to piece together the story of the Roman province are the inscriptions that proud men set up to the glory of themselves, their emperors and their gods.

A 'broch', a well-defended farmstead, at Mousa, Shetland

The task of the archaeologist is to reconstruct from all these things the lives of the people of the past, to place events in their correct order, and to find out when these events happened. If, on the site of a Roman villa, he unearths the ruins of two houses, one small and poor, the other large and luxurious, it is vital to know which was built first. If he can discover that the smaller house followed the larger, and if this same sequence is repeated in other sites, then he can guess a period of decreasing prosperity. He must then find the date of this decline, to see whether it matches the situation in other parts of the empire, and fits the facts given by the historians. Archaeologists have developed techniques to solve these problems.

As he digs down into the soil he will disclose various objects at different levels: it is obvious that the rubbish at the bottom of a well fell there before the rubbish at the top, and that a tiled floor on top of another was laid after the lower one. Sometimes separate layers can be clearly distinguished. If there is a coin in a layer – and Roman coins can be easily dated from the names of the emperors which appear on them – then we have a date *after* which the layer must have been made, for it cannot have been put down before the coin was minted. Let us see how this works in an actual example.

Roman army units used much the same building methods wherever they were stationed: if a Roman fort was damaged, the damaged section was levelled to provide a firm base for new building, which was then bonded into any parts still standing. In this rubble there may be a coin or a piece of an inscription, and almost certainly pieces of broken pottery. Now we know from literary sources that Hadrian's Wall was severely damaged and rebuilt on three occasions, in AD 196, 296 and 367. The three layers of rebuilding have been dated – for example by certain inscriptions like those from Birdoswald (on page 150) and Risingham (on page 139) – and these layers at once give dates to pieces of pottery found in them.

Pieces of pottery are often found, for our ancestors used pots where we have containers of wood and glass, cardboard, tinned-steel and polythene. The Romans used different types of pottery at different times, and these types can be recognized. When pieces are found in layers, or *strata,* which can be dated, then similar pieces will give dates to other strata in other sites. Crambeck pottery is only found on Hadrian's Wall in layers put down after AD 367, so we can be pretty certain that layers in the rest of the country containing Crambeck ware must be dated to the end of the fourth century.

A skeleton with 'his' beaker from Maiden Castle

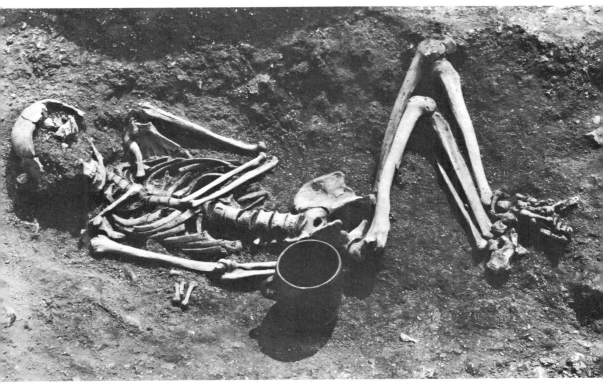

Every year we are learning how to give more accurate dates to the things found in the earth. New methods have been devised, for which the knowledge of radio-active carbon, fluorine ions and X-ray crystallography is necessary.

But we can do more than give dates to pieces of pottery. If, for instance, a tribe buries its dead in a certain fashion, and places ritual offerings or other objects with the corpse to 'help it on its way', then we can see from the tombs of the tribe how much of a country it occupied, and if it emigrated, and where to. Again, if the neighbouring tribe changed from cremating its dead to the same methods of burial, then we can guess that the first tribe had more power and influence than the second.

Let us suppose that archaeologists in 2000 years' time are investigating the

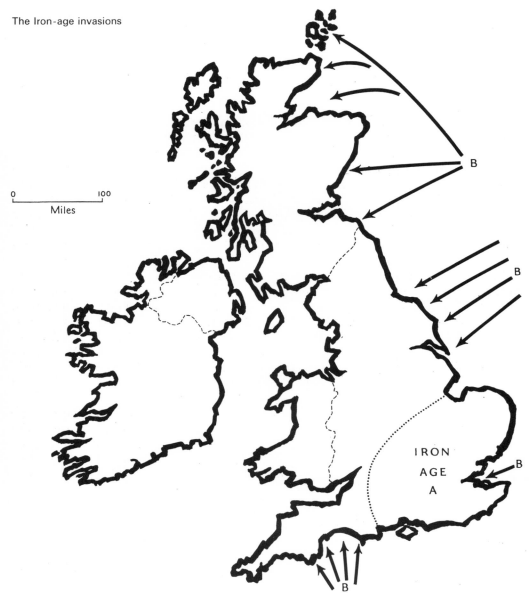

present era, and concentrate not only on pottery, but on coins, plastic goods and stainless steel cutlery as well, for all of these, like the pots, coins and metal tools of the past, are likely to survive. They will find plastic wares stamped 'Made in Hong Kong', in Europe and America, Australia and Africa, proving a trade, and *economic* connection, between these continents.

22

With them will be found coins, but only in Australia, parts of Africa and the United Kingdom will the coins bear the Queen's head: thus a *political* connection will be shown for these areas.

In China and Hong Kong they will find chop-sticks and rice bowls; in Hong Kong they will not find many stainless steel knives or dinner plates, but these will be common in the Western world: this will point to different *customs*. But dangers lie in store for them: what will they make of the plastic and china 'piggy-banks', with their hoards of coins, so common in this country? Did the English worship the pig? Similar dangers of course bedevil the archaeologist of today.

What have our archaeologists found out about the people who came to Britain before Caesar? This country has received wave after wave of invaders from the continent. The first used tools of stone, and we say that these men belonged to the 'Stone Age', which lasted from 500,000 BC until about 1650 BC. After this, bronze tools and weapons appear, and give the 'Bronze Age' its name. Although the use of iron was discovered in the Near East before 1000 BC, the first users of iron did not reach this country until roughly 500 BC. These were peasant Celtic communities from the Low Countries and France. We use the term 'Iron Age A' to refer to them.

They brought with them new agricultural methods involving ploughs with share-tips of iron, and iron bladed sickles for harvesting; they occupied the lowland, south-eastern region of England. Then came other groups, from different parts of the continent. We can distinguish them by their different tools and customs. A few of these came to south-east England, but most

The iron tip of a ploughshare, and a billhook, used by the Belgae, from Caburn in Sussex

The decorated back of
a Celtic hand-mirror

could not encroach upon land already held by tribes with iron weapons to defend it. The most representative groups went to north-east Scotland, to Yorkshire, and from Brittany to the West Country. We use the term 'Iron-Age B' when we refer to them. These were a more war-like people. The graves of the Yorkshire group contain pieces of war-chariots and horse harness; it seems likely that they bred horses, and preferred cattle-ranching to arable farming. They are the Parisi: they came from the Seine area, and the modern capital of France takes its name from *Lutetia Parisiorum*, their tribal capital.

Evidence of the character of the daily life of the West Country group is richly furnished by the lake-village at Glastonbury; it was clearly the most advanced civilisation in this country at the time. There is proof that many crafts were skilfully practised. A Celtic art had come with them, and a 'British' style of decoration developed from the continental style, from which some beautiful examples have survived.

The great hill-fortresses of Wessex, whether built by them, or as a defence against them, are clear testimony of their war-like character, also.

Celtic ornamental shield,
found in the Thames
near Battersea

The toilet articles, harness-fittings, jewels and cups found in Glastonbury and Yorkshire were much loved, and carefully preserved; these are not the wild and primitive people that Caesar believed were the inhabitants of our country.

In 125 BC there began the last series of immigrations from the continent, made by a people called the Belgae. These Belgic tribes were forced to move first by German invasions into their homeland, and secondly by Julius Caesar's campaigns, which began in 59 BC. We can trace their movements from the coins they used on the continent, and then brought with them, and from their pottery, which was made on a wheel. Three waves, using gold coins, crudely stamped and bearing no name, came from the Somme valley and Flanders along the Thames into Kent, Buckinghamshire, Hertfordshire and Essex. A fourth stream landed on the coast of south Kent and moved westward. From 57 BC onward came the Morini and Atrebates, driven from their homes by the armies of Caesar. (See map on p. 27.)

All these Belgae were accustomed

25

in the home country to live in forest clearings; they were the first people in Britain to clear away the trees, and with their stronger ploughs they exploited the heavier and more fertile soil on which the forests grew. Their forts were different, too. Leaving the hilltops they settled in valleys and on river banks, on sites which have been inhabited ever since. Caesar noticed this:

'The Britons call it a town when they have fortified a densely wooded spot with a rampart and a trench.'

The word *oppidum*, here translated as 'town', is the word Roman historians used of the hill-forts in the West Country which the Romans stormed a hundred years later.

Caesar knew about the wave of immigration into Britain which his own campaigns had caused. In 57 BC ten Belgic tribes conspired against him. Among them were the Bellovaci, the Atrebates and the Morini, all of whom issued coins in Britain. There were also the Suessiones, who

'within living memory had a king, Divitiacus, the most powerful man in Gaul, who ruled south-east Britain as well.'

Torc, or necklet, made of electrum — an alloy of gold and silver

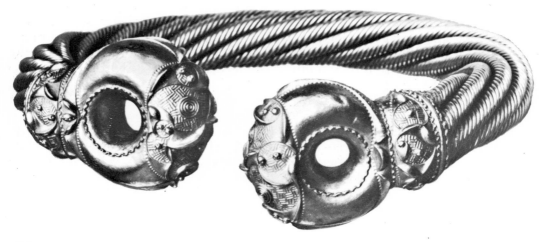

The leading tribes of Britain — Belgic tribes shaded

But Caesar soon crushed this conspiracy; in accepting the surrender of the Bellovaci he learnt that the chieftains who had inspired the resistance to him had fled:

'The guilty men had realised the disastrous results of their policy, and had escaped to Britain.'

In the belief that he had now conquered and pacified all Gaul, Caesar determined to come to Britain, to make sure that the peace he had won was not endangered by raids from across the Channel: this is the reason he gave in the very first extract. It will become clear later on that he intended more than a mere raid to warn the British not to interfere on the continent, and that he was dreaming of the conquest of the whole island. But now it is time to return to the shores of Boulogne, and to the general, impatient to be off. A few remarks of Suetonius, who wrote biographies of the first twelve emperors, are worth recording.

'He is said to have been tall, fair and well-built. His face was broad, his eyes dark and keen; he was rather a dandy, careful about shaving, and keeping his hair well trimmed. He couldn't stand his baldness, which his enemies made fun of, and so he used to brush his thin hair forward. Of all the honours voted him, the one he accepted and used most gladly was the right to wear a laurel wreath on his head at all times.'

3

Reconnaissance

In 59 BC Julius Caeser had been consul. After this, the highest civil office in Rome, he took up a military command in a province which included north Italy and southern France. Quarrels between the Gauls to the north, and an invasion by the Swiss, threatened the safety of his province; Caesar quickly made up his mind to extend Roman rule over all Gaul, for he would be strengthening his own position as well as Rome's. In 57 BC he dealt with the Belgic tribes, and appointed Commius king of the Atrebates. Next year he crushed the Veneti, who lived in north west Gaul. They had surrendered in the previous year, but, according to Strabo, they had rebelled because they had heard that Caeser intended to invade Britain, and feared they would lose their monopoly of the cross-channel trade in the west. In 55 BC the Germans had raided across the Rhine, and been driven back; Caesar retaliated with a raid into Germany. Now, late in the summer, he was ready for a quick reconnaissance, to find out what the merchants and Gauls would not tell him. It was August 25th.

'Arrangements were now complete, the weather was favourable and we cast off just before midnight. The cavalry had been ordered to make for the northern port, embark there, and follow on; but they were rather slow about carrying out their instructions, and started, as we shall see, too late. I reached Britain with the leading vessels at about 9 a.m., and saw the enemy forces standing under arms all along the heights. At this point of the coast precipitous cliffs tower over the water, making it possible to fire from above directly on to the beaches. It was clearly no place to attempt a landing, so we rode at anchor until about 3.30 p.m., awaiting the rest of the fleet. During this interval I summoned my staff and company commanders, passed on to them the information obtained by Volusenus, and explained my plans. They were warned that, as tactical demands, particularly at sea, are always uncertain and subject to rapid change, they must be ready to act at a moment's notice on the briefest order from myself. The meeting then broke up: both wind and tide were favourable, the signal was given to weigh anchor, and after moving about eight miles up channel, the ships were grounded on an open and evenly shelving beach.'

Modern plaque at Deal recording Caesar's arrival

Careful calculation of the tides on August 25–26th, 55 BC, and our knowledge of the winds that prevail at this time of year, make it more than likely that Caesar landed east of Dover, on the firm shingle between Deal and Walmer.

'The natives, however, realised our intention: their cavalry and war chariots (a favourite arm of theirs) were sent ahead, while the main body followed close behind and stood ready to prevent our landing. In the circumstances, disembarkation was an extraordinarily difficult business. On account of their large draught the ships could not be beached except in deep water; and the troops, besides being ignorant of the locality, had their hands full: weighted with a mass of heavy armour, they had to jump from the ships, stand firm in the surf, and fight at the same time. But the enemy knew their ground: being quite unencumbered, they could hurl their weapons boldly from dry land or shallow water, and gallop their horses which were trained to this kind of work. Our men were terrified: they were inexperienced in this kind of fighting, and lacked that dash and drive which always characterised their land battles.

'The warships, however, were of a shape unfamiliar to the natives; they were swift, too, and easier to handle than the transports. Therefore, as soon as I grasped the situation I ordered them to go slightly astern, clear of the transports, then full speed ahead, bringing up on the Briton's right flank. From that position they were to open fire and force the enemy back with slings, arrows and artillery. The manoeuvre was of considerable help to the troops. The Britons were scared by the strange forms of the warships, by the motion of the oars, and by the artillery which they had never seen before: they halted, then fell back a little; but our men still hesitated, mainly because of the deep water.

'At this critical moment the standard-bearer of the Tenth Legion, after calling on the gods to bless the legion through his act, shouted: "Come on, men! Jump, unless you want to betray your standard to the enemy! I, at any rate, shall do my duty to my country and my commander". He threw himself into the sea and started forward with the eagle. The rest were not going to disgrace themselves; cheering wildly they leaped down, and when the men in the next ships saw them they too quickly followed their example.

'The action was bitterly contested on both sides. But our fellows were unable to keep their ranks and stand firm; nor could they follow their appointed standards, because men from different ships were falling in under the first one they reached, and a good deal of confusion resulted. The Britons, of course, knew all the shallows; standing on dry land, they watched the men disembark in small parties, galloped down, attacked them as they struggled through the surf, and surrounded them with superior numbers while others opened fire on the exposed flank of isolated units. I, therefore, had the warships' boats and scouting vessels filled with troops, so that help could be sent to any point where the men seemed to be in difficulties. When everyone was ashore and formed up, the legions charged: the enemy was hurled back, but pursuit for any distance was impossible as the cavalry transports had been unable to hold their course and make the island. That was the only thing that deprived us of a decisive victory.

'The natives eventually recovered from their panic and sent a delegation to ask for peace, promising to surrender hostages and carry out my instructions. Their envoys brought with them Commius, who, it will be remembered, had preceded us to Britain. When he had landed and was actually delivering my message in the character of an ambassador he had been arrested and thrown into prison. Now, after their defeat, the natives sent him back.'

Caesar was probably glad and relieved to grant this request: he demanded hostages as a guarantee of British loyalty. In the next two days many hostages

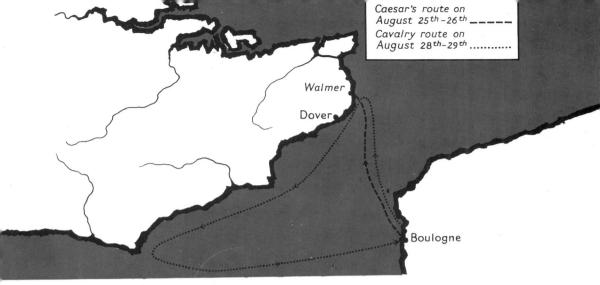

Walmer

Dover

Boulogne

Invasion route, 55 BC

were promised – only a few arrived. On August 28th, the cavalry transports at last sailed from France, and were within sight of Caesar's camp when a terrifying channel storm drove them away; only by the superb seamanship of their Gallic crews were they saved. They could do nothing except return to France. But the crews of the ships that had brought the infantry across, who were also Gauls, chose not to warn Caesar of other dangers.

'It happened to be full moon that night; and at such times the Atlantic tides are particularly high, a fact of which we were ignorant. The result was that the warships, which had been beached, became waterlogged; as for the transports riding at anchor, they were dashed one against another, and it was impossible to manoeuvre them or to do anything whatever to assist. Several ships broke up, and the remainder lost their cables, anchors, and rigging. Consternation naturally seized the troops, for there were no spare ships in which they could return and no means of refitting. It had been generally understood, too, that we should winter in Gaul, and consequently no arrangements had been made for winter food supplies in Britain.'

The British chiefs were as overjoyed as the Romans were dismayed. In the hope that, if they wiped out this expedition, Rome would never send another, they secretly re-assembled their forces and cleverly baited a trap.

'I had not yet been informed of their intention; but in view of the disaster to our shipping and the fact that they had ceased to deliver hostages, I had a suspicion of what might happen, and was prepared for any emergency. Corn was brought in every day from the fields; timber and bronze from the badly damaged vessels were used to repair others; the necessary equipment was ordered from the Continent; and thanks to the energy and efficiency of the troops, all but twelve ships were made tolerably seaworthy.

'One day while these repairs were in progress the Seventh Legion was doing its turn in the harvest field; nothing had occurred as yet to arouse suspicion of an impending attack, for many of the natives were still at work on the land and others were frequent visitors to our camp. Suddenly, however, the sentries on the gates reported an unusually large dust cloud in the direction in which the legion had gone. My suspicions were confirmed – the natives had hatched some new plot.

'The battalions on guard duty were detailed to go with me to the scene of action, two others were ordered to relieve them, and the rest to arm and follow on immediately. We had not been marching long before I noticed the Seventh was in difficulties: they were only just managing to hold their ground with their units closely packed and under heavy fire. The fact was, the enemy had guessed their destination, as the fields were already stripped elsewhere: they had hidden themselves in the woods by night, and attacked while the men were unarmed and busy reaping. We lost a few killed. The rest were in confusion before they could form up, and found themselves hemmed in by cavalry and war chariots.

'The following will give some idea of British charioteers in action. They begin by driving all over the field, hurling javelins; and the terror inspired by the horses and the noise of the wheels is usually enough to throw the enemy ranks into disorder. Then they work their way between their own cavalry units, where the warriors jump down and fight on foot. Meanwhile the drivers retire a short distance from the fighting and station the cars in such a way that their masters, if outnumbered, have an easy means of retreat to their own lines. In action, therefore, they combine the mobility of cavalry with the staying power of foot soldiers. Their skill, which is derived from ceaseless training and practice, may be judged by the fact that they can control their horses at full gallop on the steepest incline, check and turn them in a moment, run along the pole, stand on the yoke, and get back again into the chariot as quick as lightning.

'Our troops were unnerved by these tactics, and help reached them only in the nick of time: for as we approached, the enemy halted, and the legion recovered its morale. The moment, however, was clearly inopportune to precipitate a general engagement; so I advanced no further, and shortly afterwards led the troops back to camp. This episode kept us all fully occupied, and such natives as were still at work in the fields made off.

'There followed several days of bad weather, which confined us to camp besides preventing an enemy attack. But during this interval the Britons sent runners all over the countryside to inform the population that our force was very weak, and that if it could be driven from its base they had every chance of obtaining valuable loot and of securing their freedom once and for all. A strong British force of both arms was assembled and marched on our camp. It was fairly evident that what had happened before would happen again – even if we routed them, their speed would enable them to get clear of further danger. Nevertheless, there were now available some 30 horses brought over by Commius. So the legions were drawn up in battle formation in front of the camp, and after a brief action the enemy was overwhelmed and fled. We followed as far as our speed and endurance allowed, killed a large number of them, then burned all their dwellings over a wide area, and returned to base.

'That same day envoys came to sue for peace; they were met with a demand for twice as many hostages as before, and were ordered to bring them over to the continent, because the equinox was close at hand and the ill condition of our ships made it inadvisable to postpone the voyage until winter. Taking advantage of fair weather we set sail a little after midnight, and the whole fleet reached the mainland in safety.'

In Rome the news of Caesar's exploits was received with excitement: it was felt that this raid into a new and unknown land was a prelude to a full occupation in the following years. A decree was passed ordering public thanksgiving for a full twenty days, an honour never granted to anyone before. But Caesar and his men knew that disaster had only just been averted. They knew that the general's own rash and dangerous tactics were largely responsible. His reputation was at stake; he could not afford to fail again. Accordingly, as soon as he returned to France he began to prepare for next year's campaigning season.

'On the eve of my departure for Italy (a journey I had been making annually for the past few years), I directed my staff to arrange for the building of as many ships as possible during the winter and to have the old ones repaired. Detailed instructions were left for the dimensions and shape of these new vessels. To simplify loading and beaching, they were to be constructed with a somewhat lower freeboard than that commonly used in the Mediterranean, especially as I had noticed that, owing to the frequent ebb and flow of tides, the waves in the Channel are comparatively small. To allow for heavy cargoes, including numerous pack-animals, they were to be rather wider in the beam than those used in other waters; and all were to be fitted with sails as well as oars, an arrangement which was greatly facilitated by their low freeboard. Materials for their equipment were ordered from Spain.'

The whole fleet was to be ready in the spring.

A Roman warship

4

The Great Expedition

Caesar spent the winter in North Italy. Early in 54 BC he was called to Jugoslavia to defeat and punish a rebellious tribe which had been raiding into Italy. But by June he was back in France, and began to assemble a great army. He had learnt, in the last two days of his previous campaign in Britain, that Commius' cavalry, backed by the legions, could overcome chariots. This time he was anxious to run no risks: he took 2,000 horsemen. The scale of his preparations shows positively that he did not intend a mere raid to punish the tribes which had not sent the hostages they had promised: it can only mean that he intended a full-scale invasion, and occupation. But first the Channel had to be crossed.

'Soon after my arrival in Gaul I began a tour of the winter camps, and found that, notwithstanding grave shortage of materials, the troops had worked so hard that there were about 600 ships of the type described, including 18 transports, ready for launching in a few days. After congratulating the men and those in charge of the work, I gave instructions that all vessels were to assemble at Boulogne, which had been found by experience to be the most convenient starting-point for the Channel crossing, being some 28 miles from the coast of Britain'.

Then came disturbing news. One of the tribes on whom Caesar relied for some of his cavalry began to disobey orders and conspire with German forces across the Rhine. The peace of Gaul was threatened; without peace he could not go to Britain. Caesar moved at once with nearly 20,000 men and 800 cavalry; the terrified tribesmen had to give 200 hostages before Caesar could feel secure. To avoid any trouble while he was overseas he summoned the chiefs of all the tribes and ordered them to come with him so that he could keep an eye on them. Then for three weeks the weather prevented sailing; at last the wind blew fair, and the troops were ordered to embark. At that moment one of the strongest Gallic chiefs slipped out of camp and headed for home with his cavalry. The sailing was postponed, and a strong detachment was sent galloping after him. He was overtaken, and screaming defiance, 'I'm a free man, of a free country,' he was cut down and killed. His troops were brought back to the coast. Finally, on July 6th, the signal was given.

Bigbury
Walmer
Boulogne
ARTOIS

July 7th, 54 BC

'Labienus remained on the Continent with three legions and 2,000 cavalry: he was to guard the two ports, arrange food supplies, and keep an eye upon events in Gaul. Other measures were left to his discretion. Shortly before sunset I sailed with five legions and 2,000 cavalry; there was a light south-west wind, but about midnight it dropped. The tide carried us right off our course, and at dawn the coast of Britain appeared receding on our port quarter. As soon as the tide turned we rowed hard with it so as to make that part of the island where the best landing points were found last year. The soldiers worked splendidly, and by continuous rowing they enabled the heavily laden transports to keep up with the warships. The whole fleet reached Britain at about noon, but the enemy was nowhere to be seen. We therefore disembarked and chose a site for the camp.

'Some prisoners revealed that a large native force had originally concentrated on the beaches, but had withdrawn and hidden themselves at Bigbury Woods when they saw the numbers of our fleet. More than 800 ships, indeed, must have been visible at once, if one includes those which had survived last year's expedition and some privately owned vessels. We began moving inland just after midnight, leaving ten battalions and 300 cavalry under Quintus Atrius to guard the fleet. No anxiety was felt about the ships, as they lay at anchor on an open shore.

'A night march of about 12 miles brought us to the Great Stour within sight of the enemy forces. They came down with cavalry and war chariots and, by attacking from higher ground, tried to bar our passage of the river. Repulsed by our cavalry, they retired on the woods where they had a strongly fortified position of great natural strength. It had no doubt been prepared for some war among themselves, for every entrance was blocked by a mass of felled trees. Scattered parties of them came out to fight, and tried to prevent us breaking into the defences; but troops of the Seventh Legion, working under cover of interlocked shields, piled up lumber against the fortifications, stormed the position, and drove them from the woods at the cost of only a few minor casualties. I would not allow them to pursue far: the ground was unfamiliar, and I was anxious to use the few remaining hours of daylight for entrenching the camp. Early next day, however, a light force of infantry and cavalry was sent out in three columns to overtake the fugitives. They had gone some way, and only their rearguard was visible, when some troopers arrived with news from Atrius.

'It appeared that a great storm overnight had wrecked nearly all the ships or cast them ashore: the anchors and cables had parted, seamen and pilots had been helpless, and heavy damage had been suffered as a result of collision.

'After giving orders for the recall of our task force I went back to the coast, and found the news only too true: about 40 ships were a total loss; the remainder could be repaired, but it would mean a very big job. Skilled workmen were called out from the legions, others were summoned from Gaul, and I wrote to Labienus directing him to build as many ships as he could with the troops at his disposal. Meanwhile it was decided to have all vessels beached and enclosed with the camp in a single line of fortifications: it seemed the best thing to do in spite of the enormous labour involved. Actually the work took ten days to complete with the men working day and night.'

It is hard to believe that Caesar had not learnt the hard lesson of the previous summer. We can only assume that his impatience to come to grips with the Britons led him to take a risk which was to prove very expensive. The Britons saw that though his forces were now many times larger they were still subject to the same bad luck as before. The Kentish chiefs took fresh heart, but realising that they were no match for the Romans, turned for help to the most powerful man in Britain. In return he demanded, and got, the supreme command. This was Cassivellaunus, king of the Catuvellauni. He used the ten days well, and when Caesar was ready to move once more towards Canterbury, he did not advance unopposed.

'As soon as the ships were beached and the camp strongly fortified I returned inland, leaving the same guard as before, and on arrival discovered that larger British forces had assembled under Cassivellaunus. This chieftain's territory lies some 75 miles from the sea, and is divided from the coastal districts by the river Thames. Until then he had been almost continually at war with the other tribes, but owing to the general alarm inspired by our arrival they had unanimously agreed to confer upon him the supreme command.

'The enemy horse and chariots engaged in a fierce running fight with our cavalry, but we had the better of them everywhere and forced them back with heavy casualties into the woods and hills. We suffered a few losses, too, in consequence of a reckless pursuit.

'It was not long, however, before the Britons caught us off our guard during the work of entrenchment. They rushed unexpectedly from the woods, attacked the outposts which were stationed in front of the camp, and some heavy fighting ensued. The first and second battalions of two legions went to the rescue, and took up positions quite close together; but the troops were unnerved by these strange tactics, and the enemy with amazing dash broke through the gap and retreated to safety. They were eventually driven off by throwing in more battalions. That day Quintus Laberius Durus, one of our battalion commanders, lost his life.

'Throughout this peculiar engagement, which took place in full view of the camp, it was evident that our troops were too heavily armed: they could not follow up when their opponents gave ground, and they dared not abandon their regular formation. The cavalry, too, had an extremely dangerous task. Every now and then the charioteers fell back on purpose, drew them away from the legions, then jumped down and re-engaged them on foot with the odds heavily in their own favour. Besides, they never fought in close order, but always in wide open formation with reserves posted at strategic points, so that one unit covered another's retreat and fresh vigorous men took the place of their exhausted comrades.

'Next day the enemy took up a position on the hills some considerable distance from the camp. Small groups appeared and began to harass our cavalry, though with not quite the same spirit as on the previous day. However, I had sent out a foraging party consisting of three legions under a general officer, Caius Trebonius, and at midday the natives made a concerted attack, pressing right up to the companies on guard. The latter repulsed them in a furious counter-attack, and maintained pressure until the cavalry, heartened by the sight of the legions, who were moving up to their support, made a charge which drove the Britons in headlong flight and gave them no chance to close their ranks, to stand firm, or to jump from their chariots. In consequence of this defeat, reinforcements sent by the neighbouring tribes dispersed, and the Britons never again fought us in a general action.'

Caesar's belief that cavalry and infantry combined could cope with the chariots had been proved correct. He knew, though, that nothing could be achieved until he defeated Cassivellaunus in his own territory, and so moved to Brentford.

'On learning the enemy's plan, we moved up in full strength to the Thames, preparatory to entering Cassivellaunus dominions. The river can be forded at only one point, and even there the crossing was difficult. Large native forces appeared in battle order on the far bank, which was also defended by a line of pointed stakes; and some deserters in our custody revealed that more of these obstacles were planted under water in the river-bed. The cavalry were sent over first, the infantry being ordered to follow soon afterwards; but the legionaries dashed through with such speed (though only their heads were above water), that they were over as soon as the mounted troops. The Britons, overpowered by this combined attack, fled from the bank.'

Over seven hundred years later, in his Benedictine monastery at Jarrow, the Venerable Bede was to write, in a short account of this campaign:

'Cassivellaunus had stuck sharpened stakes in the bank of the river, and over almost all the ford, beneath the water. Remnants of these can be seen on the very spot even today: It is plain that each of them was as big as a man's thigh, and, set in lead, had been firmly fixed in the bottom of the river.'

One of these stakes can be seen at the Gunnersbury Park Museum, in Brentford, London.

Caesar continues:

'Cassivellaunus had now given up the idea of fighting a pitched battle. He disbanded most of his forces, and followed our line of march with some 4,000 chariots. Keeping off the main route under cover of dense thickets, he drove the inhabitants and their cattle from the open country into the woods wherever he knew that we should pass. If our cavalry ranged too far to plunder and devastate the neighbourhood they were in grave danger from native chariots sent out from the woods to engage them. In face of this threat they could not go far afield: I was obliged to keep them in touch with the main column and be content with such damage as we could do by ravaging and burning the countryside within reach of the legions.

'Meanwhile envoys had arrived from the Trinovantes, who were about the strongest tribe in that area. One of their princes, a young man named Mandubracius, had come over to the Continent and put himself under my protection: he had fled for his life when his father, king of the Trinovantes, was assassinated by Cassivellaunus. The envoys promised submission and obedience to my orders; they asked me to defend Mandubracius against the malice of

Cassivellaunus, and to send him back an independent ruler of his people. I demanded 40 hostages and a supply of grain for the troops. These were promptly delivered, and Mandubracius returned home.

'When it became known that the Trinovantes were securely protected and suffered no harm from our troops, five more tribes from southern and western Britain sent delegations and submitted. They told me we were not far from Cassivellaunus's stronghold, which was strategically placed among woods and marshland, and that large numbers of men and cattle were gathered there.

'Incidentally the Britons call a "stronghold" any densely wooded spot fortified with a rampart and trench and used as a refuge against attack by marauding bands.

'I started for this place with the legions, and notwithstanding its superb natural defences, which had been improved by strong fortifications, we proceeded to the assault on two sides. After a very brief resistance the enemy gave way and escaped on another side. Great quantities of cattle were found there, and many of the fugitives were overtaken and killed.'

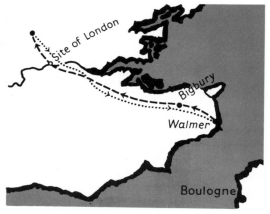

March to Cassivellaunus' fortress town at Wheathampstead, July 20 – September 25

But Cassivellaunus was not yet done. It says much for him as a man and as a general that not only did he conceive a plan, but that it was carried out, despite his defeat.

'During these operations Cassivellaunus sent envoys to the four Kentish rulers, Cingetorix, Carvilius, Taximagulus, and Legovax, directing them to make a

Part of the great ditch around Cassivellaunus' capital

surprise assault on our naval base. As soon as their forces appeared, the garrison attacked from the gates, killed many of them, took prisoner one of their leaders, a chieftain named Lugotorix, and retired without loss. The news of this engagement found Cassivellaunus already perturbed by his many reverses, by the devastation of his country, and above all by the defection of his allies. Acting through Commius, he sent a delegation to discuss terms of surrender. I had decided to winter on the Continent for fear of sudden risings in Gaul; besides, summer was nearly over, and it was clear that the enemy could easily hold out for the rest of the campaigning season: so I demanded hostages, fixed the annual tribute payable from Britain into the Roman treasury, and strictly forbade Cassivellaunus to interfere with Mandubracius and the Trinovantes. After receiving these hostages we returned to the coast. The ships had been repaired and were now launched; but since we had numerous prisoners, and some vessels had become a total loss in the recent storm, I decided to make the return voyage in two trips. It is worth noting that of the large fleets which had made so many voyages in the past twelve months not one ship with troops on board was lost. As for the empty vessels, which included those on their way back from Gaul after disembarking the first contingent, and the 60 ships newly constructed under Labienus's supervision, very few of them reached their destination: the majority were forced back to land by bad weather. We awaited them for some time in vain, until the approach of the equinox threatened to prevent our sailing at all, and there was nothing for it but to embark in what ships we had, though this necessitated a good deal of overloading. But a dead calm set in; we weighed anchor a little after 9 p.m., and the whole fleet reached land safely at dawn.'

Two things are clear. First, that Caesar was as anxious for peace as Cassivellaunus; Commius was still Caesar's ally, and must have been sent by Caesar to Cassivellaunus. The situation in Gaul had become so dangerous, that it took Caesar three years' hard fighting to quell the rebellion that broke out in the winter of 54 BC. He never had time to consider a third expedition to this island. Secondly, there is no doubt that he had failed, and that Rome knew this as well as he did. Though he had in fact met and defeated far greater forces than in his first campaign, no thanksgiving was decreed this time. The general feeling of disappointment can·be seen in the following letter, written by the Roman statesman, Cicero, to a friend in Greece.

'On October 24th I received a letter from my brother Quintus, and from Caesar, sent from the nearest point on the shore of Britain on September 25th. They have settled affairs in Britain and taken hostages; there's no booty, though they have imposed a tribute; they are bringing the army back from the island.'

5

Pause for Diplomacy

When Caesar returned to Gaul in 54 BC he had defeated the Belgic tribes of this country: their kings had given him hostages, and promised to send tribute to Rome. But he had had no time to bring Britain into the Roman Empire, and nearly a hundred years passed before the emperor Claudius was able to do so. Though we do not know many of the details of the intervening years, the main pattern of events is clear. The evidence comes not only from ancient authors, but more particularly from the many coins that were issued by the tribal kings in Britain.

The coins struck in this country first copied Gallic ones, which were themselves copies of gold *staters* minted by King Philip, the father of Alexander the Great. The drawing shows how, in successive copies, the original design deteriorated, and it is easy to see that the coins on the left were made earlier than those on the right.

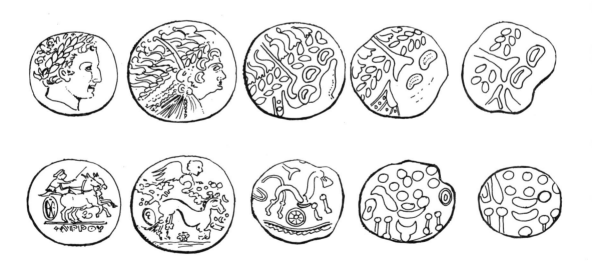

A gold stater, and Celtic copies of it

Later still Roman coins were copied, even by those tribes that actively resisted Roman influence, largely because the only other coins they saw were Roman. And so it is possible, though not always easy, to trace the relative order in which coins were minted. Moreover, as each tribe used its own special design, we can tell from where the coins are found in which areas the various tribes lived.

Soon after Caesar's death, the British kings began to inscribe their names on their coins, and so we can decide who were the kings, what areas they ruled, and roughly when they did so. Now we can consider the years between Caesar's raids and the Roman occupation of south-east Britain in AD 43.

In 51 BC Commius, king of the Atrebates in Gaul, who had joined the rebellion against Caesar, was allowed to emigrate to Britain. From the coins he issued – and he was the first person in this country to have his name inscribed on his coins – we can see that he had by 45 BC established a kingdom, with two main towns at Selsey and Silchester. So at this time the south-east of Britain, the region which had by far the most contact with Rome, was occupied by the Atrebates, who had been expelled from their homes by Roman troops, and secondly by the peoples who had formed a confederacy under Cassivellaunus and had been defeated by Caesar: all these were opposed to Rome and its empire.

But the Romans knew that all these Belgae had been defeated: in 44 BC the Sicilian historian Diodorus wrote:

'Julius Caesar . . . subdued the greatest and most war-like nations of the Celts, and extended the dominion of Rome to the Bretannic Isles.'

What had been done once could be done again. Another historian, Dio Cassius, records for the year 34 BC:

'Not to be outdone by his father, Augustus had started to lead an expedition into Britain, and had already advanced into Gaul when some of the newly captured tribes, including the Dalmatians, rose in revolt.'

We do not know why Augustus planned an invasion at this time. But in 1849 over 2,000 gold coins were found in Berkshire, known as the Whaddon Chase Hoard. An attractive theory suggests that this vast amount can only

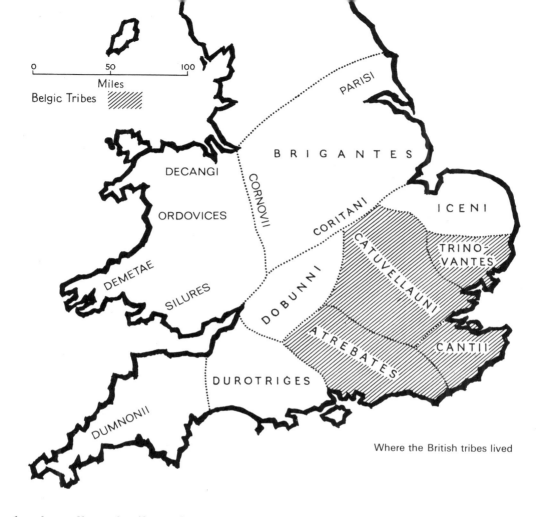

0   50   100
Miles
Belgic Tribes ▨

PARISI

B R I G A N T E S

DECANGI

ORDOVICES

CORNOVII

CORITANI

ICENI

CATUVELLAUNI

TRINO-
VANTES

DEMETAE

SILURES

DOBUNNI

ATREBATES

CANTII

DUROTRIGES

DUMNONII

Where the British tribes lived

be the collected tribute for one year, and that it was hi-jacked on its way to Rome, and hidden by the thieves, who were never able to reclaim their loot. Perhaps Augustus was planning a raid to punish the Britons for non-payment of the tribute.

Then a poem written by Tibullus in 28 BC tells us that the general Messalla was about to be sent to Britain. He can have achieved little, for Dio Cassius recounts that in the next year Augustus was planning full-scale invasion again:

'He set out to make war on Britain, but when he came to Gaul he stayed there, for it seemed that the Britons were likely to come to terms, and affairs in Gaul were still unsettled.'

45

The Celtic horse on Commius' stater

From this year also we have two poems written by Horace, almost the Poet Laureate of the emperor's court, which must surely refer to this invasion:

'Goddess Fortune . . . who can lift men from the depths, or bring down the highest at the moment of triumph . . . preserve Augustus for us when he goes against the Britons at the very end of the earth.'

and,

'We have always believed, from his thunder, that Jupiter is ruler of heaven: and Augustus, by bringing the Britons and Persians, a dangerous race, into the empire, will seem a god on earth.'

However, it seems that the British did come to terms, for Augustus stayed on the Continent: and in 25 BC he closed the gates of the temple of Janus, a sign that there was peace throughout the empire. Augustus usually preferred to achieve his ambitions through diplomacy than the use of force, and in Britain he succeeded.

Between 20 and 15 BC, Commius of the Atrebates and Cassivellaunus of the Catuvellauni both died. Cassivellaunus was succeeded by Tasciovanus, who maintained his anti-Roman policy: but Tincommius, who followed his father at Silchester, was won over by Augustus.

On the coins of Commius there is the Celtic version of a horse, which seems to have been adopted as the tribal sign of the Atrebates – other representations of it can be seen at Uffington, Berkshire, cut into the turf, and in the bronze handle found at Silchester. But Tincommius coins show a marked change: the horse is clearly a Roman horse; the name is boldly marked in

A stater of Tincommius

The Atrebate horse at Uffington, Berkshire

A handle found
at the Atrebate
capital, Silchester

Roman lettering. So one of the leading tribes was now pro-Roman, and the Cantii too favoured Augustus. Rome had nothing to fear now in Britain.

Strabo confirms this: in his book, published in Rome in 7 BC, he writes:

'Though they could have held Britain, the Romans have not thought it worth while: there is nothing to fear from the Britons – for they are not strong enough to launch an attack across the Channel – and there is little advantage in holding it. For it seems that at the moment we get more income from the customs duty than the tribute could bring in, if you deduct the cost of maintaining an army to guard the island and collect the tribute.'

And more important –

'Some of the chiefs there have won Augustus's friendship by sending ambassadors and paying court to him: they have made offerings on the Capitol, and have practically turned the whole island into a Roman province. Moreover they are prepared to pay such heavy duty, both on imports and exports – we send them ivory chains and necklaces, amber glassware and other small stuff of this sort – that there is no point in garrisoning the island; at least one legion and some cavalry would be needed to collect the tribute, which would all be consumed in paying for the army!'

This arrangement continued till AD 6, when Tincommius was expelled by his brother Eppillus, and fled to Rome. Within a few years Eppillus was in his turn driven out of Silchester by Verica, yet another son of Commius. We know that Tincommius, Eppillus and Verica were Commius' sons because they have COM.F – a Latin abbreviation for 'Son of Commius' – stamped on their coins. Eppillus then went to Kent, and took over the throne from Dubnovellaunus, who also escaped to Rome. Coin finds could tell us this;

Coin of Verica, Com F.
(son of Commius)
as Rex

Tasciovanus'
RICONI stater

but also we read in the *Res Gestae*, an account of his deeds written by Augustus in AD 7, which was inscribed on bronze tablets and posted up throughout the empire:

'Several kings came to me asking for political asylum: Tiridates and then Phrates from Parthia; Artavasdes from Persia, and Artaxares from Mesopotamia: from Britain came Dumnobellaunus and Tincommius . . .'

Augustus was not prepared to use force to restore these exiles. Instead he speedily came to terms with their successors. The coins of both Eppillus and Verica bear the Latin word REX – this indicates that they were both client kings, in treaty alliance with Rome. It was frequently Rome's policy to make a treaty with a state on the borders of the empire, and to recognise its ruler as king, so that it could act as a buffer between the empire and the barbarians beyond it.

Tasciovanus, king of the Catuvellauni, was not to be outdone. His coins too proclaim that he was king, but not in Latin. It is believed that RICONI is the Celtic word for king. And this is not the only sign of rivalry between the two tribes. The coins of Verica show a vine leaf – the wine made from vines was imported from the Roman empire. Cunobelinus, Tasciovanus' successor, has an ear of barley on *his* coins, and beer is brewed from barley – in England.

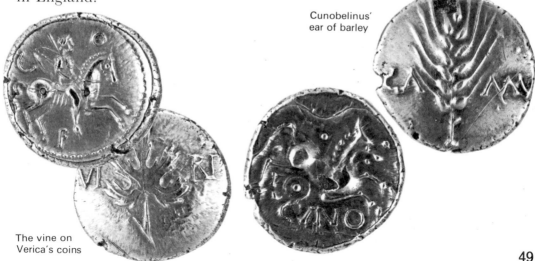

Cunobelinus'
ear of barley

The vine on
Verica's coins

49

The emperor Augustus died in AD 14: his stepson Tiberius pursued the same policy with regard to Britain, and had no thought of invasion. But the balance of power was coming down in favour of the anti-Roman party. On his succession Cunobelinus had moved his capital to Colchester and taken over the territory of the Trinovantes. In AD 25 he drove Eppillus out of Kent. The emperor Gaius, who had succeeded Tiberius in AD 37 may have been increasingly apprehensive; when in AD 40, Cunobelinus's son Adminius was banished by his father after a quarrel and fled to Gaius, the Roman emperor, who was leading a raid into Germany, thought he saw an opportunity not only to regain some of the prestige he had lost, but to settle the British question once and for all. Suetonius tells us the strange story:

'His only real achievement was to accept the surrender of Adminius, son of the British king Cunobelinus, who fled across the Channel with a few troops when his father banished him; but he sent boastful communiques to Rome, as if the whole island had surrendered to him, and told the couriers to ride right into the forum in their carriage, up to the senate house, and to hand the despatch to no one but the consuls at a full meeting of the Senate . . .'

After recounting an absurd raid into Germany, Suetonius says that Gaius moved to Boulogne:

'Finally, as if intending to bring the war to an end, he drew up his troops along the shore, and deployed the artillery; suddenly, when no one knew or guessed what he intended, he ordered the troops to collect shells, and fill their helmets and the folds of their tunics with them, calling them the "plunder won from the Ocean", whose proper place was on the Capitol or Palatine. To commemorate the victory he built a very high tower: lights were to shine from it, as from the Pharos lighthouse, to guide sailors at night. He promised each man a hundred denarii, a small present, but told them to depart rich and happy, as though he had given them a fortune.'

Whatever really happened, Cunobelinus was not much impressed by the incident. His contempt for Rome grew when he heard that Gaius had been assassinated, and that the troops rioting through the palace had come across his uncle Claudius skulking behind a curtain, and made him emperor.

Confident that he had nothing to fear from Rome, Cunobelinus, with his sons Caratacus and Togodumnus, moved into Atrebate country, and drove out Verica, who fled to Rome for help. Claudius saw that it was time to act.

The Roman historian Tacitus, writing around AD 100, sums up the whole period for us:

'The first Roman ever to take an army across to Britain was the deified Julius Caesar: he was successful enough to intimidate the people and take over a strip of land along the coast, but it is clear that he did no more than point it out to his successors: it was not his to hand over to them. Then Rome was plagued by civil wars, when our leading men took up arms against the state. Britain was long forgotten, even after peace was restored. The emperor Augustus called this his policy, while Tiberius said he was obeying instructions. We know that the emperor Gaius planned to invade Britain; but he was always changing his mind, and the failure of the great attack on Germany scared him off. It was left to the emperor Claudius to try again.'

The Invaders

Tombstone of Optio

The invasion force that Claudius sent into Britain was not very large – a little over 40,000 men. But his army experts knew that his tough, highly-trained soldiers were more than a match for the ill-disciplined hordes awaiting them.

The main strength of the Roman army lay in the infantry, enrolled in units called **legions.** There were usually about 30 legions, with between 5,000 and 6,000 men, all Roman citizens, conscripted for the most part in Italy. Every legion had a name, and a number, though sometimes several had the same number. The four that came to Britain were the Second Augusta ('The Emperor's Own'), the Ninth Hispana ('The Spaniards'), The Fourteenth Gemina (Gemina means that one legion had been formed from two others), and the Twentieth Valeria ('The Valerians'). The senior officer was the *legatus*.

In every legion were 60 **centuries,** each containing 80 men. Their officers were the *centurion*, his second in command called an *optio*, the *signifer* or standard bearer, who also acted as treasurer of the burial club, and the *tesserarius* who was responsible for the watchword. Here are the tombstones of two such officers. The centurion's

Tombstone of Marcus
Favonius Facilis

was found at Colchester: he was Marcus Favonius Facilis of the Twentieth. The optio's comes from Chester – the inscription tells us that he was Caecilius Aritus of Emerita Augusta, (a town in Spain, the modern Merida), optio of the Twentieth, who served for 15 years and died aged 34. Both are holding their staff of office.

The photograph opposite shows a life-size model of an ordinary soldier – a legionary – in the Grosvenor Museum at Chester. You can see that he was well protected with large shield and body armour. The metal strips were probably fitted to a leather jerkin by thongs loosely tied to allow easy move-ment; a scarf was worn round the neck to prevent the metal chafing the skin. He carried two javelins on the march; the shaft was of wood, the metal section was of soft iron. Only the head and the socket into which the wood fitted were hardened. He threw the javelin at the enemy from about 30 yards. The soft metal shank bent on landing: if it pierced a shield, it would be difficult to remove the clumsy thing in the heat of battle; if it fell to the ground, it would be useless to throw back.

The legionary followed up with this short stabbing sword *(gladius)*: he thrust at the face and stomach of his enemy. He did not waste time slashing, or raise his sword arm high and thus expose his right side. The sword was carried on his right side in a wooden or leather sheath. On the left was his dagger *(pugio)*, used more as a knife than for fighting. The thick-soled heavy sandals were studded with hob-nails. Next to his skin he wore a linen vest, and on top of that a woollen tunic reaching to his knees. To keep out the cold he had a rough woollen cloak.

The legionary signed on for 25 years. On discharge he received a grant of money or land. His pay was very little, and he had to pay for his own food and clothing. The fact that his food cost almost a third of his pay gives some idea of what he earned. His food was very simple – corn, made into porridge or bread, cheese and beans. He drank water, or vinegar and water, or cheap rough wine. The centurion who gave Jesus a sponge of vinegar when he was on the Cross was not being unkind; this is what the soldier drank himself.

In AD 67 a Jewish priest named Josephus was captured by the Roman army in Israel during the Jewish rebellion. In *The Jewish War*, published eight years later, he describes the army that defeated him.

'As if born holding swords in their hands they never have a rest from training. Their training is as strenuous as real warfare: every soldier every day exercises as eagerly as if he were in action. That is why they make light of fighting. No confusion drives them out of their usual formation: they are not paralysed with fear or exhausted by hard work. Victory is inevitable, for their enemies can never equal them.

'They never let the enemy catch them unawares. Whenever they invade enemy country, they never engage in battle till they have fortified a camp. They do not build it in any vague or random fashion, nor do they work all at once or haphazardly. If the ground is uneven they level it. The encampment is marked out as a square. A great number of workmen and tools are taken along with the army to build it. The interior is divided into rows of tents: from the outside the perimeter looks like a wall, and towers are spaced out at regular intervals. Between the towers they put various artillery machines for firing stones or arrows. Four gates are built into this surrounding rampart, one in each side: they provide an easy entrance for the baggage-animals, and are wide enough for the troops to dash out on quick raids in emergencies.

Model of legionary soldier

A corner of the legionary fortress at Caerleon

'The camp is conveniently divided into quarters by streets; the centre section is occupied by the officers' quarters, the exact centre by the general's headquarters, like a small temple. And so something very like a city appears, with its market place, the craftsmen's section, and the offices where the tribunes and centurions settle disputes among the men. The outer wall, and the buildings inside, are completed quicker than thought, through the numbers and skill of the workmen. If necessary, a ditch is dug round outside the wall, six feet deep and six feet wide.

'When the wall is built they go to their quarters in their tents by companies, in a quiet and orderly manner. All their other fatigue duties are performed in the same disciplined and trusty fashion, again by companies, the collection of wood and food and water when they are required. The time for breakfast or dinner is not left to the discretion of the men; they all take their meals together. The times for sleep, sentry-go and getting up are announced by trumpet-calls; in fact nothing is done without the word of command.

'At dawn the men report to the centurions; the centurions go together and salute the tribunes, and all the officers go to the commander in chief: he gives them the watchword, according to custom, and the other orders to be conveyed to the ranks. They maintain the same discipline in battle, wheeling swiftly, advancing or retreating as necessary in their units.

'When it is time to break camp, the trumpet sounds; at this signal there is instant activity. They take down their tents, and pack everything for the departure. The trumpet sounds again for them to get ready; swiftly piling their baggage on their mules and pack animals, they stand like runners at the starting line waiting for the gun. Then they set fire to the camp to prevent it being of any use to the

Plan of the Caerleon fortress

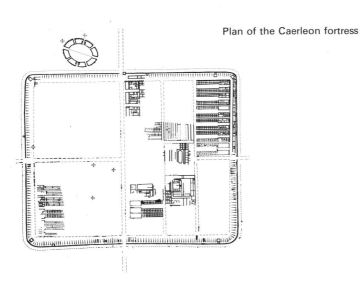

A reconstruction of
the corner of the fortress

enemy, since they can easily build another one for themselves. A third time the trumpet sounds for the departure, to hurry on those who are slow for any reason, so that no one is left out of his rank. Then the herald, standing on the general's right, three times asks in their native tongue whether they are ready for war. Three times they shout in reply, "Aye, ready," sometimes beating the herald to it, and filled with a martial enthusiasm they all raise their right hands in the air as they shout. Then they march forward, quietly in good order, each man keeping his place in the ranks, as he would in battle.'

Josephus has described a temporary camp; the earth from the ditch was heaped up to form a rampart. Sharp wooden stakes were planted in the top, bound together with ropes, and branches might be woven in and out of them for extra protection. But the permanent camps, whether legionary fortresses, or auxiliary fortlets, had a stone wall built into the front of the rampart. Huts were built of wood or stone, instead of tents. Many of these forts have been discovered in this country, and of some of them the foundations of the walls and buildings are plainly visible.

The photograph on p. 56 shows a corner of the legionary fortress at Caerleon in South Wales. You can see four barrack blocks. In each of these a century lived. Each pair of small rooms was occupied by seven or eight men in a group known as a *contubernium* – literally a 'tenting-together'. The large, irregular block of rooms at the end was occupied by the centurion and his subordinate officers; here too, of course, was the century office. The remains of two towers can be seen in the rampart; behind each of them is the cookhouse. The rings indicate circular ovens. The huge size of the camp can be seen from the plan – the longer side is 540 yards long, the shorter 460 – and some camps covered nearly 60 acres.

Outside Caerleon, and most permanent legionary fortresses, lay the amphitheatre: it was used for official or religious ceremonies, for instruction, and as a sort of sports stadium. Nearby was the bath-house: this was rather like a modern Turkish bath, with a changing room, a cold-bath room, and warm and hot sweating rooms. There were also clubrooms, where in the cheerful warmth the men sat and gossiped, played dice and boasted. The larger forts had hospitals as well, with operating theatres and rest rooms, for the medical treatment of the legionaries was of a high order.

These are the men of the legions. But only half of the invaders were

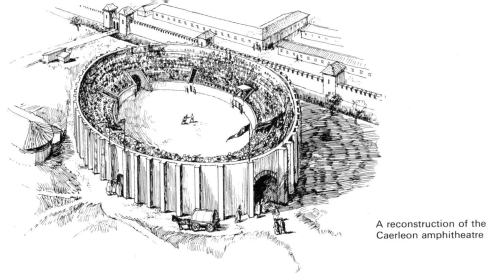

A reconstruction of the
Caerleon amphitheatre

legionaries. Most of the others belonged to the *auxilia*. These men were not usually Roman citizens, and were conscripted from the provinces of the empire. Men from Germany, Spain and Gaul, Syria and even Parthia came to serve on this island. They formed three kinds of fighting units. First, and most important, were the cavalry; mounted on small, tough horses, they wore the same helmets and breastplates as the legions. They carried:

'a large sword on their right side, and a long lance in their hands, with an oblong shield across their horse's flanks. Three or more light javelins hung beside them in a quiver, with broad heads, and as long as spears.'

The long sword and lance of the auxiliary cavalryman (see page 60) can be seen on a tombstone found at Gloucester. The inscription records that the memorial was set up to Rufus Sita, cavalry-man of the Sixth Thracian Cohort, aged 40, with 22 years service, by his heirs.

The auxilia were grouped in **cohorts** of 500 or 1,000 men, divided, like the legions, into centuries of 80 men. Cavalry cohorts were also known as 'wings', *alae*.

The auxilia also supplied infantry, but these were lightly armed, often with specialist duties; they were archers, with composite bows of steel and bone; slingers, able to fire roundshot with speed and accuracy; and swimmers, trained to swim across rivers, guiding their horses and holding their weapons clear of the water. The third type of unit provided mounted infantry, that is soldiers who rode quickly to the fighting, and then dismounted to engage on foot.

The auxilia used to fight in front of the legions, and on their flanks, to shield them as much as possible from casualties. Many battles were won by

RVFVS·SITA·EQVES·CHO·VI
TRACVM·ANN·XL·STIP·XXII
HEREDES·EXS·TEST·F·CVRAVES
H   S   E

An auxiliary cavalryman

the auxiliaries before the legions had to strike a single blow. The legionaries were highly trained men, engineers, surveyors, carpenters, masons and artillerymen as well as the foot-soldiers of the line. It is perhaps surprising that the auxiliaries were prepared to be exposed to danger first, especially as their pay was less than that of the legions; but the Roman citizenship they were awarded at the end of their 25 years' service was probably prize enough.

There were other units, too, called *numeri* or *cunei*: they came from the least civilised parts of the empire, and were not regularly organized. Inscriptions from Lancaster and South Shields tell of a *Numerus Barcariorum Tigrisiensium*: these men, with their experience of the shallow waters of the Tigris were employed on ferry service at the wide shallow estuaries of the Tyne, and in Morecambe Bay.

Last, there was the navy. It was never a very important or an independent force. Its main function was to transport and supply the army, and to keep down piracy. The British Fleet – *Classis Britannica* – was stationed at Dover and Lympne in this country, and at Boulogne in Gaul.

By AD 43 Roman legionaries, native infantrymen and horsemen, archers and engineers, Syrians, Spaniards, Italians and Gauls had gathered in north Gaul for the invasion of this country. Not very many went back.

7

Invasion

Suetonius, who wrote the *Lives of the Emperors*, did not find Claudius' invasion very impressive, or the reasons for it very important.

'The only campaign he undertook was on a small scale. The senate had voted him the triumphal regalia, but thinking this beneath his dignity, he wanted the glory of a proper triumph. Britain seemed the best place to get one: no one else had tried to conquer it since Julius Caesar's day; moreover the British kings were stirring up trouble because he had refused to send back to them a couple of political refugees.'

Only emperors and members of their families could have full triumphs, when the general and his army, preceded by their captives and carts piled high with booty, marched in procession through Rome. Other generals were granted triumphal regalia, that is the right to wear the triumphal dress and carry the laurel wreath, sceptre and crown at festivals.

Suetonius dismisses Claudius campaign in a few words. Fortunately more details can be found in Dio Cassius account.

'About this time Aulus Plautius, a distinguished senator, led an expedition against Britain. For a certain Bericus (Verica), who had been exiled from the island after a political quarrel, persuaded Claudius to send a force there, and that is why Plautius was given this command. However he had great difficulty in getting the troops to leave Gaul, as they objected to campaigning outside the limits of the world they knew. They didn't obey him till Narcissus, the ex-slave sent out by Claudius as his representative, climbed on the commander's platform and began to address them. At this they were all the more angry with Plautius, and wouldn't let Narcissus say a word. But suddenly they all yelled out the cry "Io Saturnalia", (because at the festival of the Saturnalia all the slaves put on their masters' clothes for a day's holiday) and without more ado willingly did what Plautius told them.

'But all this delayed embarkation till late in the season. They sailed in three divisions in case they found it difficult to land if they all went over together. On the way they were dismayed when they were driven back off course, but were then encouraged by a bright light which shot across the sky from east to west, the direction in which they were sailing. When they came to land they disembarked without opposition; hearing of the mutiny the Britons had not expected them to come, and so had not mustered their forces. Even after they had assembled, they did not come to grips, but hid in the swamps and forests: they expected the Romans to grow weary and sail away without achieving anything, as they had done in the time of Julius Caesar.'

The inscription at Chichester

It is not surprising that the British forces had dispersed. At least a month must have passed while Plautius tried persuasion, then sent to Rome and waited for Narcissus to drive in his carriage the length of Italy and Gaul. And so in the end the mutiny turned out to the Roman advantage. Yet in any case the Romans had planned, with the 'three divisions', to deal with opposition. The main force landed at Richborough, where the island in the Wantsum Channel, which used to cut off the Isle of Thanet from the mainland, provided an easily defended base. We can guess that the second force was a decoy, and went to Dover or Lympne. It is not unlikely that a third force should land in Atrebate country, and join the pro-Roman Belgae, and there is some evidence to support this. Built into the wall of the Council Hall at Chichester there is a large stone with the following inscription:

'This temple was erected to Neptune and Minerva, and for the prosperity of the Imperial Family, by the gild of Metalworkers and its members, at their own expense, under the patronage of Tiberius Claudius Cogidubnus, King and Imperial Legate in Britain. The site was donated by Clemens, son of Pudentinus.'

and Tacitus tells us that King Cogidubnus was granted several states in return for his loyal help. He had taken over the rule of the southern half of the Atrebates after the flight of Verica. It is probable that he was granted the titles of 'King' and 'Imperial Legate' for the help given to the Romans both now and later. If the Romans, then, landed in Cogidubnus' territory (as the inscription suggests), these precautions and plans were unnecessary, for the Britons had moved inland. Dio continues:

'As a result Plautius had much trouble in finding them, but when he did, he defeated first Caratacus, and then Togodumnus, the sons of Cunobelinus, who had died. At this time the Britons were not independent, but ruled over by the kings of other tribes. When they had fled, he persuaded a section of the Bodunni, who were subject to the Catuvellauni, to join him.'

Caratacus and Togodumnus challenged Plautius one at a time instead of waiting to join forces. Their defeats led a section of the Dobunni (Dio gets the name wrong), who had been drafted against their will from the land recently taken over by the Catuvellauni, to change sides. There can be little doubt that others soon joined them.

63

Coin issued to celebrate Claudius' triumph

'Then leaving a garrison,' continues Dio, 'he advanced till he came to a river; the Britons had encamped carelessly on the opposite bank, as they believed that the Romans would not be able to cross without a bridge. Plautius sent over a contingent of Gauls trained to swim in full equipment even across the swiftest rivers. These took the enemy by surprise, and shot and wounded the chariot horses, not the men; as a result even the charioteers couldn't escape in the confusion that followed.

'Plautius then sent over the future emperor Vespasian, and his brother Sabinus as second-in-command. This force too managed to cross the river, surprising and killing many of the enemy. The rest did not run away, though, but joined battle on the next day, still without a decisive result, until Gnaius Hosidius Geta, after nearly being captured, was able to overcome them. He was rewarded with triumphal regalia even though he had not yet held the consulship.

'The Britons retreated from there to a point near the mouth of the river Thames, where it forms a marshy lake at high tide. They crossed it easily, since they knew exactly where firm ground and the fords were, but the Romans in close pursuit were baffled by it. However the Gallic troops again swam over, while some others crossed by a bridge a little further upstream; a simultaneous attack was then made on several fronts and many of the enemy were cut down. In a reckless pursuit of the rest, the Romans rushed into impenetrable marshes, and many were lost.'

Plautius did not expect to find such little resistance at the Thames, which Caesar had found so hard to cross. The Britons cannot have left the bridge unguarded; we can only suppose that a Roman force had outflanked them and taken it, or that a joint Roman and British force had marched up from Chichester to take the Catuvellauni unawares. But Plautius had other problems; Claudius wanted a triumph, and Plautius had almost won the war before he realised it. So he tactfully paused and 'sent for help'. Dio gives us the official version:

'Togodumnus died soon after this, yet the Britons not only refused to give in, but united all the more closely to avenge him. Plautius grew alarmed and advanced no further. While keeping careful hold himself of what he had won, he sent for Claudius: he had been instructed to do this if he met opposition too strong for him. A considerable armament, including elephants, had already assembled for reinforcements.

Inscription from Claudius'
triumphal arch at Rome

'When he received the message Claudius set out. He sailed down the Tiber to Ostia, and round to Marseilles; from there by road and river he reached the Channel, sailed over, and joined the troops waiting for him at the Thames. With them he crossed the river, engaged the barbarians who had assembled to oppose his advance, defeated them and captured Cunobelinus capital, at Colchester. After this he won over many tribes, some by diplomacy, others by force, and was hailed "Imperator" several times contrary to custom – no one should receive the title more than once in any one campaign. He handed these tribes over to Plautius, after confiscating their weapons, with instruction to subdue what was left. Claudius hurried back to Rome, sending news of his victories ahead through his sons-in-law Magnus and Silanus.

'When they learnt of his success the Senate voted him the title of "Britannicus", and gave him permission to celebrate a triumph. They also decreed that there should be an annual festival, and that two triumphal arches should be erected, one in Rome, and the other in Gaul at the place from which he had set forth to Britain. They gave his son the same title, Britannicus, and this in fact became the name by which he was usually known.'

There is no trace of the arch in Gaul, but part of the one in Rome has survived; much of the inscription is lost, but we can tell, from comparison with similar inscriptions of other emperors, and with an inscription from Cyzicus recording Claudius victory, that it read:

'This arch was erected by the Senate and People of Rome in honour of Tiberius Claudius, son of Drusus, Caesar Augustus Germanicus, High Priest, Tribunician power eleven times, Consul five times, Imperator 22 times, Censor, Father of his Country, because he received the formal surrender of eleven British kings,

C

conquered without loss, and because he was the first to bring foreign nations across the Ocean under the sway of the Roman people.'

Who these eleven kings were we do not know. Prasutagus, king of the Iceni, and Queen Cartimandua of the Brigantes, both of whom we shall meet later, probably counted as two. Perhaps Cogidubnus, king of the Atrebates was included to swell the number, though his kingship was something special. His lands, with the capital at Chichester, became known as *Regnum,* the Latin word for kingdom, and his people as *Regnenses* – 'the king's people.'

It must have been an impressive sight when Claudius moved into Colchester, perhaps with his elephants, strange and frightening to the cowed British, for the formal surrender. He was justly proud of the sixteen days which Dio tells us he spent in the country, and liked to remember his success. Suetonius tells us:

'Wearing his general's cloak he presided over a tableau he put on in the Campus Martius of the assault and sack of a town, and the surrender of the British kings.'

Colchester was at first the leading town of the new province: it was chosen as the site of the great Temple of Claudius, intended to be the religious centre of the country.

But one question remains: what was happening while the army waited by the Thames for Claudius? Suetonius supplies part of the answer:

'In the reign of Claudius, Vespasian was appointed to Germany as a legionary commander: this was due to the influence of the freedman Narcissus. He was transferred from there to Britain, where he fought 30 battles. He beat two of the strongest tribes, captured over 20 towns, and subdued the Isle of Wight, under the command of Aulus Plautius, general of the expeditionary force, and also while Claudius was in command.'

Since Vespasian was in Rome by AD 44, he must have been busy in AD 43! Archaeological evidence gives the rest of the answer.

The recent excavations at Fishbourne near Chichester, have revealed, in addition to the magnificent palace of King Cogidubnus, some timber

Multilated skulls
from the war graves
at Maiden Castle

Roman ballista bolt
in Briton's spine

buildings, almost certainly military granaries. In 1966, near the east gate
of Chichester, a large army camp was found, probably the army base for the
march west. And in the West Country, excavations at Hod Hill, where
a Roman camp was later built in the corner of the British earthworks, at
Spettisbury Rings, at Ham Hill in Somerset and at Maiden Castle in Dorset,

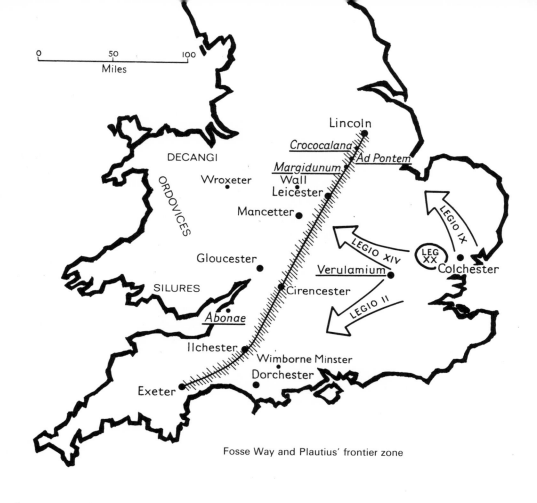

Fosse Way and Plautius' frontier zone

have revealed the grim effectiveness of Roman weapons. At Maiden Castle a Roman ballista bolt was found embedded in the *front* of a vertebra after passing through the body, and mutilated skulls show the work of the Roman sword.

Plautius had made good progress in a short time; and by AD 47 he had conquered south-east Britain. A frontier zone stretched from Devon to the Wash, and a road linking its various sectors had been built. The map shows this road, the Fosse Way, and the places where forts or other objects have revealed the presence of the Roman army in these early days. Plautius had brought four legions with him – the Second Augusta, the Ninth, the Fourteenth and the Twentieth; their movements too are indicated. The base camp at Colchester was held by the Twentieth Legion. The Ninth advanced

68

towards Lincoln, where its first permanent camp was established six or seven years later. The Fourteenth probably operated in the Midlands with a base at Wall, and the Second spent these early years in the West Country; in 1967 archaeologists excavated what was almost certainly its base – a large 42 acre camp at Wimborne Minster.

Aulus Plautius was given an ovation when he returned to Rome in AD 47, the first person outside the imperial family to receive one for 66 years. Claudius went out to meet him when he entered the city, and courteously gave him the place of honour up to the Capitol and down again. Claudius and Rome were proud of what had been done in Britain. A poet of the time did not exaggerate too much when he wrote:

'There is an island, Britain, far away across a distant sea, surrounded by harsh and rocky shores. The sea-god hid it behind impassable waves, and Ocean washes it with treacherous tides. The climate is cold and wintry, the Great Bear never sets. Claudius Caesar had only to glance at it, and it was conquered and enslaved, though always free before. Now every race can meet there: now it is part of our world though once a world apart.'

8

Expansion

Aulus Plautius was followed in AD 47 by Ostorius Scapula. The historian Tacitus, writing about AD 113, tells of his five years as governor. Tacitus wrote a history of the Roman Empire up to his own day in two great works: the *Annals* covered the years AD 14–68, and the *Histories* AD 69–96, but unfortunately long parts of these are missing.

The account in the Annals dealing with Britain begins with the arrival of Ostorius Scapula. The leader of the British forces is Caratacus, last heard of before the Medway battle. We do not know what he had been doing in the next four years, but at some time he had fled to Wales, and assumed command of all the forces opposed to the Romans. To do this he must have had the support of the Druids. These were Celtic priests, with great influence over the British chieftains, mainly because they were responsible for the education of the chiefs and their sons. The headquarters of the Druids in Britain were to be found in the Isle of Anglesey.

'In Britain, the governor, Ostorius, had to deal with a chaotic situation. Hostile tribes poured into the province, with all the more enthusiasm because they were sure that the new commander would not move against them, when he neither knew his troops nor had any time left before winter. But Ostorius was aware that his first actions would decide how the enemy, and his own men, were to regard him. He hurried out with some auxiliary units, cut the opposition to pieces and chased away the remnants. In case the peace should be so uncertain that there would be no rest for himself or his men, and to prevent the enemy rallying again, he determined on two courses – to disarm everyone he could not completely trust, and to extend the conquest to the rivers Trent and Severn.'

The map shows the new area of operations. But the advance was not free from trouble. The Iceni, a client kingdom which had so far remained in peaceful alliance with the Romans, did not trust Ostorius's plan to disarm them. In AD 48 they rebelled, and were quickly joined by the neighbouring tribes. But they were soon crushed; Ostorius did not even have to bring up the legions. In this action his son won the Roman equivalent of the Victoria Cross. Ostorius was now able to think of retaliation for the

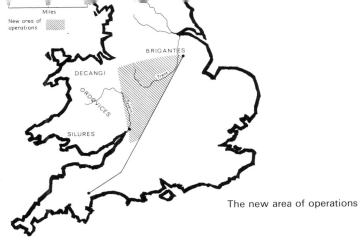

The new area of operations

raid into the province which had greeted his arrival. In AD 49 he advanced into north Wales; we must presume that this had been the base for the enemy raid.

'The army was launched against the Decangi, burning their crops and driving off their cattle. The enemy did not dare fight in the open, and when they tried an ambush were punished for their trickery. Ostorius had almost reached the Irish Channel when he was recalled by an uprising amongst the Brigantes: he had made up his mind not to push forward until the land already conquered was quite secure. The Brigantes, for their part, subsided when the rebels were killed and the rest pardoned. But the Silures were not affected by his treatment whether harsh or lenient. They plunged into war, and a legionary camp had to be built to subdue them. To facilitate this a strong colony of discharged soldiers was founded in conquered land at Colchester, to help not only in preventing revolt, but also in making the people familiar with legal government.'

By the end of AD 49 a large number of legionaires were due for discharge. These were forced into retirement at Colchester; they were probably not very happy, for only a few years before they had mutinied at the thought of coming to this country at all. Ostorius needed new troops: the *colonia* of veterans would take over the guard duties of the Twentieth Legion stationed at Colchester and free it for service on the front. Then the Fourteenth moved toward Wroxeter – its Latin name was *Viroconium*, and Wrekin comes from it – with its base camp probably near Lichfield. This camp grew into the Roman town of *Letocetum* at Wall. This and other sites occupied by the Roman army in the first few years are marked on the map on page 68.

In the Spring of AD 50 Ostorius was ready to advance into Silurian country in south Wales. Naval squadrons operated in the Bristol Channel to support him. Near Lynmouth on the Devon coast two small signal

71

stations at Martinhoe and Old Burrow have been excavated. Coins of Tiberius and Claudius show that they were almost certainly used at this time; the charred remains of the signal fires were also found.

'Ostorius then marched against the Silures. In addition to their natural ferocity they were relying on the prowess of Caratacus; he had fought many battles, and though he had not won them all, he had never been defeated. He was consequently the leading British general. His forces were inferior, but his knowledge of the country gave him tactical superiority. He transferred the war to the country of the Ordovices, (Ostorius had probably drawn the net tightly round him in south Wales during the campaigning season of AD 50), and, joined by all those who were afraid of a Roman peace, he staked everything on a last battle (early AD 51), choosing a site for it where every feature, every path, favoured him and hindered us. On one side were steep hills; the gentle gradients on the other were blocked by rocks piled up into a rampart. In front flowed a river, difficult to cross; groups of armed men were positioned outside the defences.

'The chieftains went round their men, encouraging and reassuring; among other heartening words, they said there was little to fear and much to hope for. Caratacus strode here and there, and swore that this day and this battle would lead either to the recovery of their liberty – or everlasting slavery. He reminded them of their ancestors who had driven out the dictator Caesar, and whose courage had saved them from Roman officials and Roman taxes, and preserved in safety their wives and children. The mob burst into cheers at this, and every man swore by his tribal oath not to give in to swords or wounds.

'The Roman general was dismayed at this enthusiasm, and alarmed by the obstacle of the river, the rampart that had been built, the overhanging crags and numbers of fierce warriors. But his soldiers demanded the chance to fight, shouting that nothing could resist their courage; their officers said the same, and increased their eagerness. So Ostorius, after inspecting possible approach routes, led his enthusiastic soldiers forward across the river without difficulty.

'At the rampart both sides hurled their javelins, and we suffered the heavier casualties in killed and wounded. Our men locked their shields over their heads to form a "tortoise", broke down the rough barricade, set to work with their swords on equal terms, and drove the natives to the hilltops. Close behind them ran our men, the light-armed auxiliaries attacking with their spears, the legions in close order. The British lines were thrown into confusion, for they had no

72

'Tortoise' from
Trajan's Column
(left-hand section)

helmets or breastplates to protect them. If they stood up to the auxiliaries, the legionaries' swords and javelins cut them down; if they faced the legions, they fell to the broadswords and spears of the auxiliaries.

'It was a famous victory. Caratacus's wife and daughter were captured, and his brothers surrendered. He himself sought refuge with Cartimandua, queen of the Brigantes. But there is no escape for the defeated; he was put in chains, and handed over to the Romans. This was the ninth year of the war. His reputation was not confined to Britain, but had reached the provinces: he was even talked about by the Italians. They longed to see the man who had for so long defied our power. Even in Rome his name counted for something, and the emperor, in exaggerating his own glory, increased the fame of his captive.

'The people were summoned as if to a great spectacle, and the Guards were drawn up on parade outside their barracks. First in the procession came Caratacus's subordinates, then his decorations, neckchains and the booty won in wars with his neighbours; next on show were his brothers, wife and daughter; last the king himself. In their fear the others made humiliating entreaties, but Caratacus held his head high, and when he mounted the dais made no appeal for mercy, but said,

' "If my success had been anywhere near as great as my breeding and my rank,

I would have come to Rome as a friend, not a prisoner, and you would not have despised a peaceful alliance with the ruler of many nations, a man nobly born. But my present situation is as degrading as yours is glorious. Are you surprised that I am loth to lose the men and horses, the arms and wealth I used to have? Should everyone welcome slavery, just because you want to rule the world? If I had surrendered without a fight before being brought here, my ill-luck and your success would have both passed unnoticed. They will be forgotten if you punish me, but if you spare my life, I shall be an everlasting proof of your humanity." And at this Claudius pardoned him, his wife and his brothers.'

What were the feelings of Caratacus on the slow journey through Gaul to Italy, as the crowds on the way poured out to see him? What were his impressions as he gazed on the great aqueducts and amphitheatres of Gaul and Italy? A partial answer comes from Zonaras, who wrote in Byzantium nearly four hundred years later:

'A foreign prince, Caratacus, was captured and brought to Rome. He was pardoned by Claudius, and, while walking round the city after his release, was gazing on its splendours and size: "Why on earth," he said, "when you have all this, do you want our miserable tents?"'

Ostorius was called to Rome and honoured for his victory. But if he hoped, when he returned to Britain, for more and easier successes, he was sadly disappointed. Tacitus tells of the events of AD 52.

'Ostorius was granted triumphal regalia, but from then on he met with less success. His troops were perhaps not so enthusiastic, believing that the war would soon be over as Caratacus was gone; possibly the enemy, in pity for their king's fate, burnt with an even greater desire for revenge. In Silurian territory . . . the fighting never stopped. Guerrilla warfare in the forests and marsh country was the order of the day; battles were fought by chance, or followed courageous planning, for revenge and for booty, with orders and without.
    'The obstinacy of the Silures was extraordinary; they heard of a remark of the Roman general to the effect that they must be completely wiped out, and this roused them to fury. When they began to urge other tribes to join the revolt, giving them presents of plunder and prisoners, Ostorius died, exhausted by the

weight of his responsibilities. The Britons were overjoyed that such a famous general had been killed by the strain of the war, even if not in battle.'

While the army was without its leader, the Silures plundered far and wide, and even defeated a legion, until checked by the arrival of the new governor, Aulus Didius. We know little of the next eight years. We can safely presume that the legionary camps at Gloucester, Wroxeter and Lincoln were maintained, and that the outposts were garrisoned. In any case it is not likely that the Romans would have been anxious to push forward. In AD 54 Claudius had been murdered; for some time the young Nero who succeeded him even contemplated a complete withdrawal from Britain. Moreover there was trouble again from the Brigantes, probably in AD 56.

'Since the capture of Caratacus, the best general on the other side was Venutius, the Brigantian. He remained loyal and under our protection while married to Queen Cartimandua, but after divorce attacked both her and us. At first they fought amongst themselves, and Cartimandua cunningly captured Venutius's brother and relatives. But her enemies were spurred on by the thought of the disgrace of being ruled by a woman, and in their fury invaded her kingdom with a picked band of young warriors. But we had foreseen this possibility, and had sent in a detachment to help her. A fierce battle was fought, and the result was long in doubt till final victory. Another battle, equally successful, was fought by a legion (the Ninth) under Caesius Nasica, for Didius was old and tired. He had no desire for further honours, and thought it good enough to act through subordinates, not personally, and to keep the enemy out of the province.

'All these events took place over several years under two governors, but I have put them together here. They would have been hard to remember if I had related them separately.'

Nero eventually decided not to withdraw from Britain, and sent younger, more active generals to extend the conquest. The only accounts we have are in two brief summaries which Tacitus wrote of the early years of the province. Here is one of them from the biography he wrote of his father-in-law, Agricola, who was to become Britain's most famous governor.

'The first governor, of consular rank, was Aulus Plautius, and next Ostorius Scapula, both fine soldiers. Gradually the part of Britain nearest Gaul was shaped into a province; on top of that a colony of veterans was founded. Cogidubnus, who remained a most loyal ally up to modern times, was granted certain states: it is an old and well established custom of the Roman people to use even kings to keep others enslaved. Then Didius Gallus consolidated what his predecessors had won, and even pushed out a few forts into the interior; he hoped in this way to get a reputation for enlarging the province. Veranius took over from Didius, but died within a year. Then Suetonius Paulinus had two successful years, in which he both conquered some tribes and built some forts. This success encouraged him to attack the island of Anglesey, which was sending reinforcements to the rebels; in so doing he left himself open to an attack in the rear.'

A reconstruction of the palace of King Cogidubnus

9

Boudicca

Suetonius Paulinus spent his first two years in Britain making sure of the land already occupied by the Romans, and advancing into central and northern Wales. The Silures still held out in the south, but in the north the last centre of resistance was the Isle of Anglesey. Tacitus relates what Suetonius did; the year was AD 60.

'He therefore planned to attack the Isle of Anglesey: it was not only thickly populated itself, but had also offered refuge for those who had fled Roman power. For the infantry he built flat-bottomed boats to cope with the treacherous shallows; the cavalry made their way over by a ford, or swam beside their horses in deeper water. A dense mass of armed men lined the shore to oppose them. In and out of their ranks ran women – like Furies they were dressed in black, with dishevelled hair, and brandished blazing torches. Behind stood the Druids, lifting their hands to heaven, and shrieking awful curses. The weird sight paralysed our men. They stood there unmoving, and made no attempt to defend themselves.

'Then Suetonius shouted encouragement, and urging each other not to be scared of a pack of women and madmen they advanced, cut down everyone they met, and rolled them back into their own altar fires. Afterwards a garrison was set over the conquered island. They cut down the groves devoted to their sacred rites, for the Druids thought it proper to drench the altars with the blood of their captives, and to consult human entrails to find out the will of their gods. But while Suetonius was arranging this, news reached him of a sudden revolt.'

The news was from East Anglia, and caught the general unawares. He had with him the Fourteenth Legion and part of the Twentieth, and a good proportion of the auxiliaries. The rest of the Twentieth and part of the Second Legion was held down by the Silures, and was too hard pressed to be spared. Only the Ninth at Lincoln remained in striking distance of the revolt; the British had timed the rising well. The reasons for it are clear.

Claudius had made grants of money to several British tribal leaders to encourage them to build better and bigger towns. When Prasutagus, king of the Iceni, died he left part of his property to the emperor, hoping in this

Model of Temple of
Claudius at
Colchester

way to satisfy any claims the Romans may have had on his people. But the
financial administrator, called a *procurator*, Catus Decianus, demanded all
the grants back, as if they had been loans, and treated all Icenian territory
like captured land. When Prasutagus's widow Boudicca (she used to be
called Boadicea) protested, her daughters were raped and the queen was
flogged. It was too much for the Iceni. They sprang to arms, and were
immediately joined by the Trinovantes and some other tribes which still
cherished independence.

'They particularly hated the veterans who had not long before been settled in the
colony at Colchester. They robbed the natives of their houses and land, and
called them "prisoners" and "slaves". The soldiers encouraged this lawlessness;
their own behaviour was no better, and they hoped for the same indulgence
themselves later on. Moreover the Temple of Claudius seemed to the British a
sign that they would never be free, and the men chosen as its priests had to
waste all their money in its service. It seemed easy to destroy the colony; Roman
commanders had neglected to provide it with defences, concerned more with the
pleasures of the place than what it needed.'

Tacitus next records some mysterious events, obviously carefully stage-
managed by the Trinovantes to terrify the inhabitants of the colony.

'At this time, for no clear reason, the statue of Victory at Colchester fell down,
with its back turned as if running away. Women were thrown into a frenzy, and
prophesied destruction, and declared that the cries of barbarians had been heard
in the senate house, that the theatre had re-echoed with shrieks, and that a
mirage of the colony had been seen, upside-down, in the Thames estuary. The sea
turned blood red, and as the tide went out objects like corpses were left behind.
All this brought hope to the Britons, and fear to the veterans.

Head of Claudius, perhaps
torn from the temple statue

'Suetonius was miles away, so they asked the procurator for help. He sent barely 200 men, not properly equipped either. There were a few troops stationed there as well. But the Romans did not build a rampart and ditch, or evacuate the old people and women, for they relied on the temple to defend them. Moreover, some of their British friends were secret supporters of the conspiracy, and confused their plans. With misplaced confidence, as if peace prevailed, they allowed a horde of natives to surround them. In the attack everything was broken down or burnt, except the temple. The soldiers concentrated here and held out for two days. Then it was sacked.

'Petilius Cerialis, commander of the Ninth legion (at Lincoln) raced south to the rescue, but the victorious Britons routed his legion and killed all the infantry. Cerialis and the cavalry got away to the legionary fortress and took shelter behind its walls. Catus Decianus was appalled at the catastrophe and the hatred of the provincials; it was his avarice which had driven them to war. He fled across the Channel to Gaul.'

As soon as Suetonius heard of the revolt, he ordered most of his infantry to march towards the south-east, and sent instructions to the Second Legion, based at Wimborne Minster, or perhaps by now at Gloucester, to join him somewhere on the way. As it happened, its commander was with him in north Wales; its camp commandant, an ex-centurion named Poenius Postumus, was in temporary command, a mischance which was to have disastrous results. Suetonius himself hurried ahead with the cavalry. But the Second Legion failed to meet him. Poenius had weighed the chances – and stayed where he was.

'But Suetonius, with admirable resolution, pressed on through the enemy to London. This town had not been honoured with the title of "colony", but was an important commercial centre. At first he thought of making it his base for the war; but he saw how few men he had with him: Petilius had acted rashly and been shattered. On this evidence he took the decision to save the whole province by sacrificing this one town.

'He gave the signal for departure, undeterred by the tears and lamentations of those who implored his aid, but he did allow everyone who could keep pace to join his ranks. Those prevented from leaving by sex or age, or who could not bear to desert their homes, were overwhelmed by the enemy. The same disaster

79

overtook the *municipium* (a term that implies its official recognition as a *Roman* town) of Verulamium (St. Albans). Intent only on plunder and the easiest way to get it, the natives by-passed small forts and garrisons, and hurried to where the loot was richest and the defences weakest.

'It has been established that roughly 70,000 Roman citizens and their allies were put to death in the places I have mentioned. The British did not bother to take them prisoner, to sell them as slaves or ransom them: as if determined to exact vengeance before they were forced to pay the penalty, without a moment's delay they hanged them, crucified them, cut their throats or burnt them at the stake.'

Suetonius now rejoined the Fourteenth and the detachments of the Twentieth, (the rest he had left in north Wales to prevent it, if possible, from joining the rebellion) collected the nearest auxiliaries, and decided to seek a quick end to the war in a pitched battle. Though greatly outnumbered, he could rely on the vastly superior discipline and training of his men. The site he chose for the battle has not been identified, but was probably somewhere along Watling Street: a spot near the village of Mancetter is the most likely suggestion.

'He chose a position in a narrow valley, with a wood behind him. He could thus be sure that the enemy was not in his rear, and that the open ground in front was free from ambush. In the centre were the legionaries, in tight array; on each side of them were the auxiliaries, and the cavalry was on the flanks. The bands of British infantry and cavalry, on the other hand, wandered all over the field in unprecedented numbers. They were so confident that they brought along their wives to see their victory, and set them in wagons at the circumference of the battlefield.'

It was the practice of ancient commanders to address their troops before leading them into battle with rousing speeches of encouragement; it was the practice of ancient historians to record those speeches, or, in most instances, to make them up, writing what they thought would be suitable in the circumstances. Tacitus and Dio Cassius both give us the speeches of Boudicca and Suetonius, on this occasion, but they do not sound very realistic. We can, though, imagine Boudicca driving past the varied detachments of the British tribes in her chariot, with her daughters in front of her.

'She was,' says Dio, 'a huge woman, with a piercing glance and strident voice: a mass of chestnut hair hung below her waist. Round her neck was a great golden torque. She wore a full, flowing tartan dress, and over it a thick cloak, fastened by a brooch. She never wore anything else. On this occasion she grasped a spear, to terrify everyone.'

Tacitus reports the battle. His father-in-law was there and will have told him all the details. Though Tacitus omits all these, we can, in his few sentences, feel the grim ferocity of the struggle.

'The general's speech aroused such enthusiasm that the old hands, so experienced in battle, longed to hurl their javelins. Sure of success, Suetonius gave the signal. At first the legionaries stood unmoving, letting the narrowness of the valley protect them. Then with unerring aim they launched their javelins as the enemy came up close, and burst forward themselves in wedge formation. The auxiliaries did the same, and the cavalry with levelled lances shattered any pockets of resistance. The rest of the enemy turned tail; but escape was difficult, for the wagons they had stationed blocked their path. Our soldiers killed their womenfolk as well. Even the oxen, transfixed with spears, added to the heaps of dead.
    'It was a great victory, as fine as any in earlier days. One report said that nearly 80,000 Britons were killed, but only 400 of our men died, with a slightly larger number wounded. Boudicca took poison. Poenius Postumus, camp commandant of the Second Legion, learnt of the success of the Fourteenth and Twentieth. Because he had robbed his legion of the chance of equal glory, and against all the rules had disobeyed his general's orders, he stabbed himself to death with his sword.'

It had been a dreadful summer. Many thousands had been cruelly slaughtered – three towns had been plundered and fired. Signs of the savagery, though few, can still be seen. In London, near Lombard Street, a layer was found, red from the burnt clay and daub of the timber houses, and containing fragments of the pottery of this date, burnt black. It was two feet thick. Seventeen bronze coins of Claudius were found 15 feet down, seared by the heat.
    In Colchester, the evidence is clearer. Several sites have been found in which various objects can date the burnt buildings quite certainly to 60 AD.

When a new café was being built in 1927, a seam of Roman pottery and glass was discovered. The pots had been stacked at the time of the fire, and shelves of glass above them had melted and dripped onto the pottery. In a cellar next to the Red Lion in the High Street over 400 pieces of plain and decorated pottery were brought to light, which must have come from an early shop. Twenty-seven burnt coins of Claudius and Agrippa were unearthed on the site of the Telephone Exchange. In 1953 blocks of burnt alabaster were found: they came from the great temple of Claudius, in which the veterans died.

At St. Albans, the Roman town of Verulamium, when Bluehouse Hill was widened in 1957, a black layer of burnt ash and timber was found, contrasting with the bright red clay and daub. At another site a block of wooden shops had been rebuilt in the same manner as those destroyed. Perhaps the owner survived the holocaust, and came to live in the town again.

Layer of burnt ash and clay at Verulamium

The Boudicca group on the Thames Embankment

But the best reminder of these stirring events is the memory of Boudicca herself. Poets, playwrights, historians and sculptors have been inspired by her story. She has become a symbol of gallant patriotism. In one flight of fancy it was suggested that Stonehenge was her grave, and today she rides high in her sculptured chariot by the Thames Embankment. But in truth the rebellion she led was soon crushed, even if at great cost. However the province was rebuilt with skill and care, as we shall see, and the new province was all the finer and stronger than the one she destroyed.

10

Recovery

The backbone of the revolt had been broken. Suetonius and his men, horribly embittered by the sight of the burned and tortured corpses of Roman women and children, could think of only one course – punishment and vengeance.

'And so,' says Tacitus, 'the whole army was brought together and kept under canvas to finish the war once and for all. The emperor Nero increased the numbers of the troops by sending from Germany 2,000 legionary soldiers, eight cohorts of auxiliaries and 1,000 cavalry: by their arrival the Ninth legion was brought up to strength, and the auxiliary infantry and cavalry were stationed in new winter quarters. Every tribe which had rebelled, or had been unreliable, was battered down by fire and the sword. But the greatest hardship endured by the British was famine. In conscripting every man, young and old, for the war, they had not bothered to sow crops, expecting to use Roman supplies instead.'

But Suetonius's policy was hopelessly shortsighted: hatred only bred hatred and yet more fighting. One man at least realised this. The new procurator, Julius Classicianus, urged that the past should be forgotten and the province rebuilt in a spirit of co-operation and mutual help. It is not surprising that Suetonius and his men scorned the idea, or that Tacitus, prompted by his father-in-law, was equally hostile to Classicianus.

'The obstinate British were too slow to accept peace, because Julius Classicianus, Catus's replacement, disagreed with Suetonius's policy, and let this personal quarrel interfere with our national interests. He had spread the word that they should wait for a new governor, who would be free from anger or pride since he had not himself fought or conquered them, and would treat them mercifully if they surrendered. At the same time he reported to Rome that there was no hope for an end to the fighting unless Suetonius was superseded: he said that the governor's present difficulties were due to his viciousness, and his past success to good luck.'

Classicianus's judgement that ruthless vengeance would never bring back peace or prosperity was of course right, and made Nero anxious to discover the truth.

Classicianus'
tombstone

'Therefore Polyclitus, one of the imperial freedmen (ex-slaves: compare the incident of Narcissus on page 61) was sent to investigate. Nero was confident that Polyclitus's influence would be enough to reconcile the governor and procurator, and induce the natives to think of peace instead of rebellion. Polyclitus played his part and travelled with a most impressive retinue – very expensive for the Italians and Gauls. In Britain his progress overawed even our own troops, but the enemy laughed at him. They were still independent, and did not yet know how powerful the freedmen were: they were astonished that the general and army which had won so great a war should pay attention to a slave.

'Everything in the report to Nero was toned down. Suetonius was retained, to carry on general administration, but when, some time later, he lost a few ships and their crews on the coast, on the pretext that he was unable to conclude the war he was ordered to hand over the command to Petronius Turpilianus, who had just been consul. Petronius left the enemy unmolested, and they did not challenge him; he applied the honourable word "peace" to what was lazy inactivity.'

But Nero's estimate of Petronius's handling of the province was different. We know nothing of what he did; yet he must have restored a firm peace which allowed the island to recover. When he was recalled to Rome after his two years' of office in AD 63 he was awarded the triumphal regalia, an honour which was *not* granted to Suetonius. But the real hero of the whole story is Classicianus: he had the courage to stand up for the British people against the anger and power of Suetonius and his soldiers. There is no mention in history of any reward for Classicianus. But by a strange chance we do know that he continued in office, and died in this country. In 1852 part of his tombstone was found on Tower Hill, and in 1935 nearly all the rest was recovered. It now stands in an honoured position in the British Museum.

The next governor was Trebellius Maximus. In his six-year term of office he encouraged peace with equal success. Trouble came to him, not from the British, but from his own soldiers. They found their inactivity boring: in AD 66 the Fourteenth Legion, which had been honoured after defeating Boudicca with the titles *Martia, Victrix* – the Victorious, Fighting Fourteenth – was recalled to Italy for a campaign in the East. Perhaps it could be genuinely spared, perhaps it had caused too much trouble. Tacitus tells of an incident which may be connected with it.

'Trebellius had no energy, nor any military experience, and governed the province with a courteous kindness. The natives in turn learnt to turn a blind eye to vices so long as they gave pleasure, and the intervention of our Civil Wars provided a fair excuse for doing nothing. But a mutiny broke out when our soldiers, accustomed to hard campaigning, ran riot in peacetime. Trebellius ran away and hid, to avoid meeting his angry army: with his dignity and self-respect gone he could only make requests, not give orders. The mutiny petered out harmlessly, when a bargain was made in which the general saved his life by allowing the army to do what it liked.'

· The Civil Wars mentioned by Tacitus occurred in AD 68 and 69. After Nero had been driven to suicide, no less than four men in turn – Galba, Otho, Vitellius and Vespasian (the man who had stormed Maiden Castle) – from various parts of the empire were encouraged by the armies they commanded, fought for the throne and became emperor. AD 69 was known to the Romans as 'The Year of the Four Emperors'. But according to Tacitus:

'No passions were aroused in the army in Britain. Indeed no other legions behaved more loyally throughout the whole period of the Civil Wars. They were far away, and cut off by the Channel. Another reason may be that their frequent campaigns had taught them to reserve their hatred for the enemy.'

This remark is made at the beginning of the first book of the *Histories*. But toward the end of the same book he has another story to tell. The legions in Germany promised support for Vitellius:

'There was no hesitation in Britain either. The governor, Trebellius Maximus, was hated and despised by the army for his greed and meanness. He was made even more unpopular by the actions of Roscius Coelius, legate of the Twentieth Legion. They had long disliked each other, a feeling which the Civil Wars intensified. Trebellius accused Coelius of disobedience and stirring up trouble – Coelius pointed out that the legions had been deprived of the chance of booty, and were penniless. This scandalous quarrel of its commanders ruined the army's discipline: the situation got so far out of hand that the auxiliary infantry and cavalry also denounced Trebellius, deserted him and went over to Coelius. Trebellius fled to Vitellius. However, the province stayed quiet, even without its governor. It was controlled by the legates of the legions; in theory they had equal power, but his bold action gave Coelius supremacy.'

The next governor was Vettius Bolanus; the Fourteenth Legion was sent back with him.

'As the Civil Wars had not finished Bolanus did not cause trouble in Britain by enforcing discipline. Still no action was taken, either against the enemy or the army's slackness. The difference was that Bolanus was a decent man, and had done nothing to cause unpopularity. Everyone liked him, even if they did not respect him.'

The inactivity that Tacitus criticises had in fact wiped away the horrors of rebellion. When trouble did break out, in Yorkshire, the south-east stayed quiet.

'These quarrels (of the four emperors) and the many reports of the Civil Wars gave the Britons fresh heart. They were led by Venutius: he was naturally a violent man, and loathed everything Roman, but in addition he was spurred on by a personal animosity for Queen Cartimandua. She ruled the Brigantes, and was well born and powerful; her influence grew stronger when, by treacherously

Vespasian

surrendering King Caratacus, she added lustre to the emperor Claudius's triumph. This had brought her wealth, and with prosperity came a taste for refinement. So she divorced her husband Venutius, and chose his squire Vellocatus to share with her both marriage and the throne. The scandal immediately endangered the royal household. Venutius was supported by the Brigantian people, Vellocatus by the queen's love – and ruthlessness.

'So Venutius asked his neighbours for help; a simultaneous revolt among the Brigantes brought Cartimandua to a desperate plight. She asked us for protection, and our auxiliary cavalry and infantry did rescue her from danger by dint of some hard fighting. Venutius kept the kingdom, and we were left with the war.'

This is the situation, graphically described by Tacitus, which it seems that Bolanus preferred not to interfere in further. But when he was replaced in AD 71, the new emperor Vespasian, remembering his own days in Britain, determined on a new advance. He sent a man of action, the Petilius Cerialis who had raced so bravely from Lincoln in an attempt to save the province from Boudicca, and had been so severely handled for his pains. At the same time he sent a new legion, the Second Support Legion, to replace the Fighting Fourteenth, which never came back to Britain.

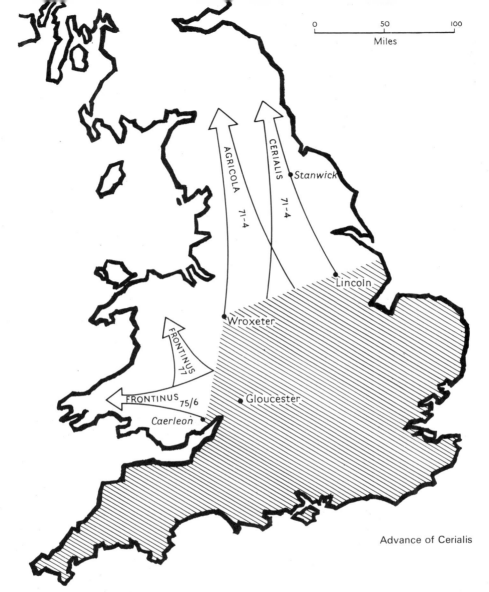

Miles

AGRICOLA 71-4

CERIALIS 71-4

•Stanwick

•Lincoln

Wroxeter•

FRONTINUS 77

FRONTINUS 75/6

Caerleon•

Gloucester•

Advance of Cerialis

'When Vespasian took over control of Britain together with the rest of the empire, there came a series of great generals and first-class armies. The enemy's hopes dwindled to nothing. Petilius Cerialis at once reduced them to terror by an attack on the Brigantes, said to be the largest tribe in the country. There were many battles, and often many casualties: most of Brigantia was conquered or devastated.'

89

Fortifications at Stanwick

Though the Silures in Wales were still unconquered, Petilius left this task for later governors, and moved north in two columns, commanded by himself and Agricola. He transferred the base of the Ninth Legion from Lincoln to York – he reached Carlisle, as pottery finds of this period indicate –, and three large marching camps discovered between York and Carlisle may be his. But little more was known of his movements till Sir Mortimer Wheeler excavated the great hill fort of Stanwick, near Scotch Corner, in 1951. There seems little doubt, that this massive fortification was built soon after AD 43, and then twice enlarged till its defences stretched for over three and a half miles. These were hurriedly finished, and then almost immediately systematically knocked down, and levelled. This cannot be anything but the camp of Venutius, large enough to contain all his Brigantian supporters and their possessions. Here he went in AD 56, and from here thirteen years later he swept down on Cartimandua. And here again he made his last stand against Cerialis and the Ninth.

When Cerialis was relieved, in AD 74, the emperor granted him a second consulship, only four years after his first. This great honour shows how highly his victory over the Brigantes was valued in Rome, and marks him as one of the finest governors.

'Indeed Cerialis would have overshadowed the work and reputation of any other governor; but Julius Frontinus succeeded, and maintained the same level. No ordinary man could have surpassed his achievements. He forced the powerful and war-like tribe of the Silures into submission, and the difficulty of the country was as hard to overcome as the bravery of the enemy.'

Frontinus was an engineer, a surveyor and author: we still have the book he wrote on the aqueducts of Rome, and a collection of *Stratagems,* useful dodges for outwitting the enemy. He believed that the Welsh problem must be finally settled before Scotland was invaded. He moved the Second Augustan Legion from Gloucester to Caerleon, which became the great military fortress whose ruins we can see today. He brought in the Second Support Legion, and the Twentieth from Chester. He pushed roads into the hills, to Abergavenny (Gobannium), to Y Gaer in Brecon, and past the gold mine at Dolau Cothi to Cardigan Bay. He built auxiliary cohort forts, well supplied, well sited and virtually invincible, which kept watch in winter over what he had won in the summer. Coastal forts, which could be provisioned by land and sea, arose at Carmarthen and Neath. Such an assault the Silures, for all their bitter fighting, could not endure. At last they sued for peace. They were allowed to build a tribal centre – *Venta Silurum,* modern Caerwent – but it always remained one of the smallest tribal capitals: the Romans had long memories.

Frontinus moved north to wipe out the very last resistance, put up by the Ordovices in north Wales. But he was recalled before he had the chance to succeed. The task was left to the greatest of Britain's governors, Gnaius Julius Agricola. The biography which Tacitus wrote of him is an invaluable record of the early years of the province. But before we come to the climax of the conquest we must consider one of the important features of Roman administration, which made the conquest possible.

11

Roads

When the Romans marched inland in the first days of the invasion they used the trackways made by the Britons; they swam the rivers, or waded through shallow water. But tracks and fords were not good enough for the constant traffic of troops and equipment. And when peace came and trade flourished – when the British 'corn, cattle, gold, silver and iron', which Strabo expected, was carried to the coasts, and Italian traders brought their wares to tempt the Celts – proper roads and bridges were needed instead of mud and marsh.

The main river barrier was the Thames. The engineers who were to build the permanent bridge looked for a place where the river would be narrow enough and the soil suitable. When they found a small trading post, built over gravel beds reaching right up to the river bank, their search was over. The small settlement in time became the great city of London.

From it roads were constructed to all parts of the country. The first consideration was for the army, to enable the troops to march quickly from the base camps to the frontier, or to deal with sudden emergencies. Soon, when traders swarmed into the country close behind the troops, roads were made so that the produce of the country could be collected and exported, so that wine and warm clothes, new boots, nails and cement could reach the forts of the legions and the new towns which the Romans founded and encouraged.

To transform the new territory into a recognisable province of the empire it had to be 'romanised', and the most effective way to do so was to provide it with towns. For towns were the basis of the Mediterranean civilisation which Rome was anxious to impart to the rest of the world. A province could be most easily organised through sensible use of the towns, and in them the laws could be administered and the taxes collected. Without them there would be no markets or trade from which came the profits the Romans sought. But towns would not be built in the first place, or lived in and visited when they were built, unless good roads joined them to their neighbours and to the capital. It was the combination of first-class roads and busy towns that made the scattered, separate and isolated tribes of the country into one unit – the *Provincia Britannica*.

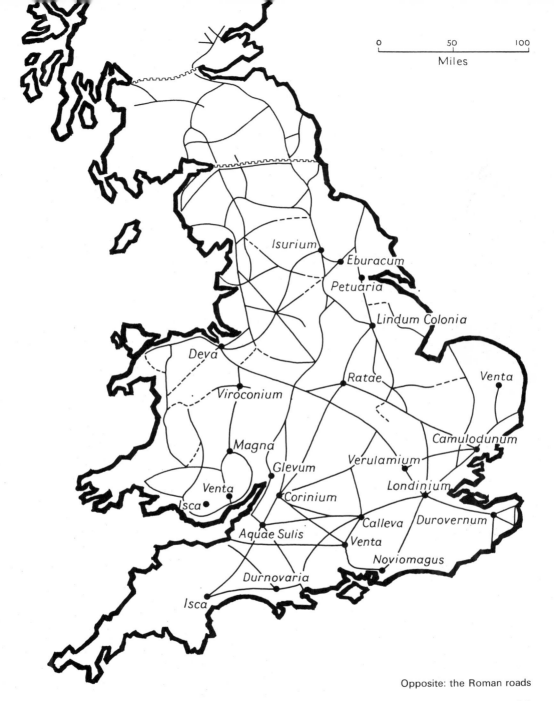

Isurium

Eburacum

Petuaria

Lindum Colonia

Deva

Ratae

Venta

Viroconium

Camulodunum

Magna

Verulamium

Glevum

Londinium

Venta

Corinium

Isca

Calleva

Durovernum

Aquae Sulis

Venta

Noviomagus

Durnovaria

Isca

Opposite: the Roman roads

93

A typical Roman road

Metalled surface
with 5" camber

Gravel
layer

Foundation of rough stones

Drainage
ditch

0   5   10   15   20 feet

Much of the hard work of road-building was probably done by labour gangs of captured Britons, but the engineers, surveyors and skilled craftsmen came from the legions.

First the general line of the road had to be determined. Without maps or compasses the surveyors took sights from one high point to the next: to find the alignment in flat, wooded country they watched for the smoke rising from fires lit by their men. These intermediate marks were moved to and fro until the surveyor was satisfied that he had chosen the shortest, straightest route that was practicable. Roman roads are famed for their straightness, but they are not absolutely straight. They are made up of long straight sections, with small but abrupt bends on high points from which the sightings were taken. There are detours round obstacles; a road will move across the slopes of a valley to decrease the gradient. But once the obstacle is passed, the road usually rejoins the original alignment. The Roman road-builder accepted much steeper gradients than are common today; but we must remember that marching men in a hurry will prefer a short steep climb to a long trudge round a hill.

Next the trees or turf were cleared, and in most cases a firm embankment was raised so that the road might have a properly drained base. Pits or ditches were dug and the earth from these was piled up into the embankment. These ditches can sometimes still be seen, but often over the centuries they have filled up, and are now invisible. The great size of the *agger* – the Latin word which we still use for these embankments – is frequently puzzling. When there is least need of it, on a high open moorland for example, it is often enormously wide and high. It has been suggested that the agger was built high to impress the natives, to form a boundary, or to satisfy the whim of the man in charge of the construction; but we do not really know.

The foundation of the road was then laid on the agger, normally big stones, carefully placed. On top of this were layers of smaller stones, sometimes cemented together, then small flints or gravel rammed down hard to form the surface. Local materials were used. At Blackstone Edge in the Pennines the road was paved with stone slabs: specially squared and dressed blocks were laid in a centre strip, and the ridge worn in it by the brakepoles of the wagons can still be seen. In the Weald of Kent the slag from the iron mines was available, and this has rusted into an incredibly hard surface, where the term 'metalling' seems particularly suitable.

Leeming Lane (Durham)

Road at Wheeldale Moor, Yorkshire

But there is no hard and fast rule. At some places the agger on the main roads is huge. On Ermine street it is frequently four or five feet high and 40 to 50 across. Sometimes it is hardly more than a slight swelling in the ground. The surface layer may be barely an inch thick, or over two feet, though this may merely be the result of lazy repair work, where layer has been laid on layer. Nearly always there is a considerable camber, and the fall from the centre of the road to the side may be as much as one foot in eight. The Roman engineers were well aware how important it was that the rain should drain quickly away, and not lie in puddles.

The main roads are usually 24 feet wide, though a few may extend to 30 feet. Minor roads vary between 15 and 18 feet, while the smallest are only from 10 to 12. But there is one dimension that is consistent. The marks and ruts worn by the wheels of the carts and wagons have been found on some of the road surfaces we have uncovered, and these are more clearly visible in the gateways of towns and forts. It seems clear that the standard Roman wagon had its wheels about 4 feet $8\frac{1}{2}$ inches apart. Once this gauge was fixed it was unlikely to be changed – no one would want to ride with one wheel in a rut and the other out. It was convenient, and did not alter over the years; eventually it was adopted by the railways, and has survived till today.

Occasionally, parallel with the road, small ditches, only one or two feet deep, have been noticed. They seem to have defined the outer limits of the road 'zone' – an area cleared of any scrub and trees that might harbour wild animals, bandits or even enemy troops. The fact that they are almost always either 84 or 62 feet apart indicates a division between major and minor roads even then. But these ditches are so small that on cultivated ground they have usually disappeared, and only in high remote areas can traces of them be seen.

By the end of the first century a network of roads covered most of the country, to Hadrian's wall and beyond. The map shows how well the Roman surveyors had explored our land: a comparison with a map of our modern trunk routes reveals at once that our transport system, road and rail, is based on the Roman. And this is not really surprising; then, as now, London was the largest and most important town, and nearly all main roads led to it. There were few roads like the Fosse Way which cut across the country. The pattern of the roads reflects the series of advances west, north-west and north made by the invading army.

Along the main roads were 'posting stations'. There was a postal service organised by the state for official communications, but not for private letters. At regular intervals the state established couriers, with teams of strong post-horses; letters were passed from one posting stage to the next. The postal service, *cursus publicus*, was important, and under the care of specially appointed officers.

Stane Street, the road from Chichester to London, had four posting stages, at Hardham, Alfoldean, which have been excavated, and probably at Dorking and Morden. Any modern government or Forces establishment is surrounded by a wall or tall wire fence to keep out the general public. The Roman army and courier service were equally jealous of their property, and surrounded it with the ancient equivalent of barbed wire – ditches and ramparts. The Latin name for these posts was *mansio* – 'a place to stop' – from which the word 'mansion' comes. The *mansio* at Silchester, where five roads met, was large, 200 feet by 210 feet, twice as big as any private house in the town, with its own bath house.

For over 300 years the roads served the province well. But in AD 410 the Roman army was withdrawn to the continent, and the administration with it. Though the Roman way of life did not disappear for many years, there was no central government to insist on the maintenance and repair of the roads. Bridges fell to pieces and potholes grew bigger and bigger. When the Saxons stayed here, the roads deteriorated even more quickly, for the new settlers were independent and self-supporting farmers. They did not need towns or markets, they did not need the roads.

However the agger still rose above the surrounding fields; the Saxons called it a 'high way'. In many places the stone surface of the roads survived, and to this the name 'streat' was given; these are of course the origins of our

Groove worn in the road at Blackstone Edge, Lancashire

'highway' and 'High Street'. Though the Saxons did not travel on the roads, they used the high embankments as the boundaries between their farms and villages. This is why modern parish boundaries so often follow the lines of the old Roman roads; indeed many of the roads have been discovered from this fact, when they were not visible before.

On the disused roads grass and weeds grew; millions of worms brought their casts to the surface, and the roads disappeared beneath the soil and humus, wind-blown dust and seeds. When a slope is ploughed, the earth gradually moves downhill, and in this way, too, many a metalled surface was concealed. When, through Norman and Mediaeval times, traffic slowly increased, the surface and then the foundations of many roads wore right away; in some places long, hollow tracks appeared instead. As small sections became waterlogged and impassable, detours were made round these bogs, and straight roads turned into winding lanes. Finally, from the age of the stage-coach and the turnpike, some of the old road system was rebuilt; the highways were levelled and made wider, and eventually vanished beneath tarmac and concrete.

12

Agricola

The steady advance of the army, and the pauses for romanisation had drawn all but a tiny fraction of England and Wales into the Roman province of Britain. The man who was to carry the conquest further than anyone else, right into north Scotland, was Gnaius Julius Agricola. If the biography written by his son-in-law Tacitus had not survived he would be nothing to us but a name, but by a lucky chance we can still read the full story of his life. He is an excellent example of the hundreds of fine administrators who lived and died in the service of Rome.

He came from a highly successful middle-class family, though not from Rome or even Italy. He was born only three years before Claudius invaded Britain, at *Forum Julii,* a colony in south-east Gaul planted by Julius Caesar for his veterans. It is today the small town of Fréjus, which was devastated in 1959 when a dam burst in the hills above. His grandfather had been a procurator, like Classicianus, and his father had risen to be a senator in Rome. At the age of 21 Agricola fought against Boudicca under Suetonius Paulinus, as a junior officer. Then his political career prospered in Rome. He came back to Britain as *legatus* of the Twentieth Legion under Cerialis, and commanded one of the columns pushing into the lowlands of Scotland. Promotion took him as governor into Aquitania, one of the 'three Gauls', until AD 77, when he became consul. After that, probably in AD 78, he crossed the Channel a third time, as governor of Britain.

Tacitus briefly describes the events leading up to his arrival. Cerialis had overcome the Brigantes and probed into Scotland; Frontinus had crushed the Silures, and when he was recalled, was on the point of advancing against the Ordovices; they did not waste the opportunity.

'This was the military and political situation,' says Tacitus, 'which Agricola encountered when he reached Britain. Over half the summer was gone; the soldiers, as if that year's campaign had been given up, had their minds on securing for the winter, while the enemy were looking for an opening. A week or two before his arrival the Ordovices had almost entirely annihilated the cavalry cohort stationed in their territory: as a first step it had excited the province. The anti-Roman party welcomed this lead, and waited to see how the new commander would react to it. The summer was over, the auxiliary units were scattered throughout the province, and the legions assumed that there would be no fighting that year – all circumstances which hardly favoured a quick campaign. Moreover most people advised him that it was better merely to keep a watchful eye on the suspected district. Despite all this, he determined to go out and face the danger.

'He assembled some detachments from the legions, and a few auxiliaries. Because the Ordovices did not dare face him in level country, he took his men up into the mountains. He himself led the way, to lend the rest some of his own courage by sharing the risks. He wiped out the whole tribe, almost to a man; but he was aware that he could not allow the prestige he had won to waste away, and that the greater his first successes were, the greater terror he would inspire in the future. So he made up his mind to annex the Isle of Anglesey. I mentioned earlier that Paulinus had been called away from occupying it by the rebellion of Britain.

'There were no ships available, as the plan had only been formed at the last moment, but the resourcefulness and determination of the general got his men across. He picked the best of the auxiliaries, who knew about rivers and had learnt from childhood to swim without losing control of their weapons or horses. When they stripped off, he sent them across so quickly that the enemy were stupefied. After expecting a fleet and ships, and an attack from the sea, they realised that an army that could swim to war could overcome anything. So they asked for terms and surrendered the island.

'Agricola's reputation soared; at the very moment he had entered office, when most officials are engaged in ceremonial visits and parades, he had undertaken a hard and dangerous operation. Moreover he did not boast of his triumph; to keep in check a tribe already conquered was hardly, he said, a "campaign" or a "victory"; even his despatches carried no "victory laurel leaves". But by denying fame he made it all the greater. A man who made light of such a considerable success was expected to go very far indeed.'

The campaign was probably not as important as Tacitus makes out; but Agricola did not waste his good luck. Adopting Frontinus's policy against the Silures, he pushed roads and forts into the interior of north Wales. He planned to control the whole country from a quadrilateral of forts at Caerleon, Carmarthen, Caernarvon and Chester. All were accessible by sea, and he ordered new roads to be built to link them to the main road system. The

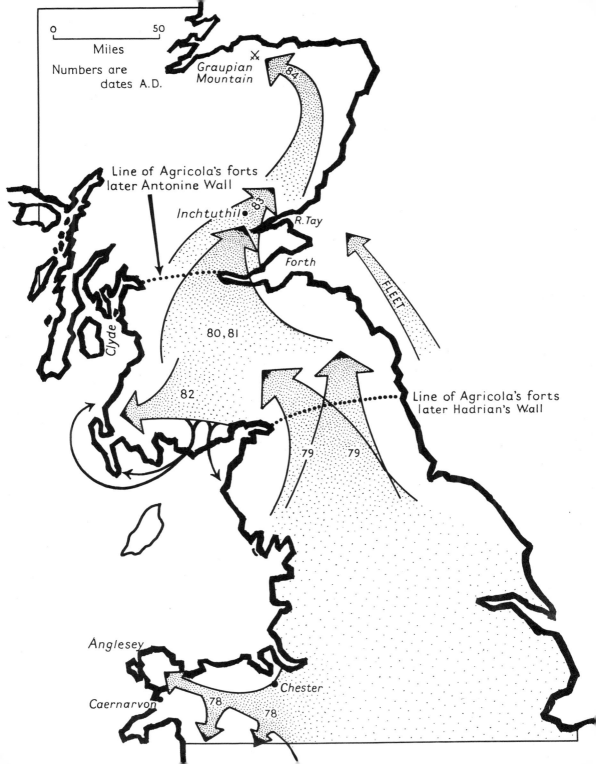

O   50

Miles

Numbers are
dates A.D.

Graupian
Mountain

84

Line of Agricola's forts
later Antonine Wall

Inchtuthil

83

R.Tay

Forth

FLEET

80,81

Clyde

82

Line of Agricola's forts
later Hadrian's Wall

79   79

Anglesey

Caernarvon

78

78

Chester

plan was a complete success; the Romans had no more trouble from Wales.
While his plans were being put into effect, Agricola had other problems to solve.

'Agricola knew how the provincials felt, and seeing from the experience of others that an unjust administration undid any success won by the army, he resolved to eradicate the causes of war. Beginning at home he first put his own staff in order; that task is as difficult for most people as governing a province. No official business was left to slaves or freedmen. He did not promote a soldier or centurion as a result of personal feeling, recommendation or petition, but thought the best man would give the best service. He knew everything that happened, but often turned a blind eye. Small offences he pardoned, serious crimes he dealt with severely. Penitence satisfied him more often than penalties. He tried to appoint honest men to positions of responsibility to avoid having to punish the dishonest.

'He eased the burden of taxation by distributing it fairly, and cut out the profitable rackets which the British objected to more bitterly than taxation. They had been forced to play a grim game, waiting at granary doors which never opened to buy back their own corn at ludicrous prices. They were told to deliver the corn to distant places by devious routes; tribes with permanent camps nearby had to send it to remote camps off the beaten track; what could have been reasonable for everybody became a source of profit for a few.

'He stamped out all this in his very first year, so that peace became something desirable – the lack of understanding and patience of his predecessors had made it as detestable as war. When summer came (AD 79) he concentrated the army; he was often with his men on the march, praising their discipline or chivvying the stragglers. He was the man who chose the sites for their camps and reconnoitred the forests and rivers. He gave the enemy no rest from sudden plundering raids. When he had reduced them to terror he reminded them of the advantages of peace by sparing their lives. As a result many tribes, up to that time fiercely independent, gave hostages and accepted peace; the garrison forts were positioned so carefully and methodically that this part of Britain was added to the province with less trouble than any before it.'

Since Wales had been dealt with, it is clear that the 'many tribes' must belong not only to Cumberland and Westmorland but to southern Scotland as well. The Stanegate, a road running across England just south of Hadrian's

INCHTUTHIL
Fendoch
Dalginross
Bochastle

Newstead

Corbridge
Stanegate

Catterick

YORK

CHESTER

0   50
Miles

Great Casterton, a Roman fort discovered by aerial reconnaissance and subsequently shown by digging to belong to the Claudian period. Ditches round the southern half of the fort are visible in terms of 'crop marks'.

wall, and the forts at Corbridge and Newstead, for example, were built by Agricola at this time. He was in fact taking over the country he had explored earlier under Cerialis.

Tacitus tells us that he spent the next winter in England accelerating the policy of romanisation. But this is a topic we shall deal with later. In the summer of AD 80 he returned to Scotland.

'New nations were discovered in the campaigns of the third year, and raids were made as far north as the estuary of a river called the Tay. This display of force so scared the enemy that they did not dare to attack the army, even though it was buffeted by appalling weather. There was even time to build some new forts. Experts observed that Agricola's use of natural features was unequalled; no fort whose site he chose was ever stormed, surrendered or abandoned. A year's supply of corn protected them against long sieges, and the winter held no fears for the troops. With a secure base for themselves they made frequent raids until the enemy were baffled and gave up hope. They had in the past made up for their losses in the summer by their successes in the winter, but now they were hounded all the year round.'

Many of the Agricolan forts have been discovered recently from aerial photographs. Ancient ditches and walls, normally invisible beneath the soil, can often be traced from an aeroplane in a dry summer. Crops and grass grow higher and greener over a ditch, for the disturbed soil which fills it absorbs water more easily, and has a higher proportion of humus, while in the shallower soil over buried stonework they quickly become stunted, parched and brown.

'Agricola never took the credit for other men's achievements; any officer high or low could rely on his unbiased testimonials. According to some reports his reprimands were too severe, and he *was* as unpleasant to rogues as he was courteous to decent men. But once his anger was past no secret resentment remained, so that there was no need to fear his silences. It was better, he thought, to hurt a man than to hate him.

'The fourth year (AD 81) was spent in consolidating the new territory; if the courage of the army, or the glory of the Roman name, had permitted, the province of Britain need have been extended no further. For the waters of the Clyde and Forth are carried far inland by the tides of the seas to east and west, and only a narrow strip of land separates them. This strip was now secured by garrisons; the whole stretch of land to the south was ours, for the enemy had been transported (across the rivers) into what was almost another island.'

The line of the two rivers, when the land between was fortified, would have been a very convenient northern frontier for the province: in fact it *was* the frontier when the Antonine Wall was built, probably along the line of Agricola's forts, 60 years later. Archaeological evidence to confirm this is scanty, and certainty is impossible, but it seems likely that the sites of the forts at Cadder, Camelon, Castlecary, and possibly Croy Hill and Bar Hill, were first chosen by Agricola.

In the following year Agricola did not advance northward; it seems likely that a decision had been taken in Rome that enough men and money had been spent. Did Agricola write to the emperor that 'the courage of the army and the glory of the Roman name' demanded that they should go on to the end of the island? If so his appeal was granted, as we shall see in the next chapter. But while waiting for the emperor to deliberate, and the answer to arrive, Agricola probably probed west into Galloway.

'At the start of his fifth year of campaigning Agricola took part in some amphibious operations; in a series of successful engagements he subdued some tribes till then unknown. He deployed troops along the coast of Britain facing Ireland, but not with defence in mind. He hoped rather that Ireland – it is halfway between Britain and Spain, and equally accessible from the Gallic Sea – might link together the parts of the strongest section of the empire with great advantage to each.

'It is quite small compared with Britain, but larger than the islands of the Mediterranean. It is very like Britain in its soil and climate, and in the character of the people and their way of life. A good deal has been learnt about its harbours and approaches from traders who sail there for business. After a civil war one of the Irish princelings was banished; Agricola gave him asylum, and kept him, under the guise of friendship, in case he should prove useful. He often said to me that one legion and a few auxiliaries could conquer and hold down the country; it would also help our relations with the Britons if Roman arms were on every side, and liberty were nowhere to be seen.'

But Agricola's advice was never taken, nor did the Romans ever go to Ireland. One wonders how a single legion and a few auxiliaries would have fared with the independent Celts who have stoutly resisted any form of invasion from that day to this.

13

Into the Highlands

After waiting a year on the Clyde–Forth frontier, and exploring south-west Scotland, Agricola was ready to press forward again from his line of forts:

'In the summer in which his sixth year of office began (AD 83), Agricola overran the people living beyond the Forth. He was worried by a general unrest in the north and some ominous movements of an enemy force, and sent his fleet to reconnoitre the harbours. He was now for the first time employing the fleet (which had in the past merely transported the army) on offensive operations, with remarkable effect, since the war could be hurried on by land and sea simultaneously.

'Often infantry, cavalry and marines, together in the same camp, shared their rations and their entertainment; they capped each other's stories of their deeds and adventures, and with typical boastfulness compared the dangers of storm and tide with the perils of the forests and mountains, the conquest of the seas with a victory over an enemy on land. Prisoners confirmed that the sight of the fleet dumbfounded the British too; they supposed that their last refuge in defeat was closed to them now that the secrets of their seas were disclosed.'

It is in this period that the series of forts north of the Clyde–Forth line was built, culminating in the great legionary fortress at Inchtuthil.

'The inhabitants of Scotland turned to armed resistance in great strength, which was, naturally, exaggerated as accurate information was lacking. Their unprovoked attack on a small fort was even more alarming. Disguising their cowardice as "strategy" some men advised Agricola to withdraw across the Forth of his own accord before he was driven across. But at that moment information came that the enemy were about to attack on several fronts. In case their local knowledge and superior numbers enabled them to get behind him, he advanced himself, dividing his force into three groups.'

Three of the forts, at Bochastle, Dealginross and Fendoch, guarded the mouths of the valleys. The British would have to eliminate them in order to

Fort at Ardoch

cut Agricola's communications. He took his men to strengthen the forts. The enemy decided to deal with his columns one by one:

'When they learnt this (that he had divided his army into three) the enemy quickly changed their plans, reunited, and made a night attack on our weakest group, the Ninth Legion. They broke in while our men were asleep, killing the guards in the first confusion. The fighting was still going on right in the camp, but Agricola, informed by his scouts of the enemy's route, had followed on their tracks. He ordered his fastest cavalry and infantry to attack them in the rear, and told his whole force to shout out the battle cry all together. The standards gleamed in the first light of morning. Caught between two fires the Britons were terrified. The men of the Ninth regained their courage; no longer afraid for their lives they could fight for glory. They even threw the enemy back, and there was a terrible struggle in the narrow gates till the enemy was beaten. One of our groups fought hard to prove that they had brought help, the other to show they had not needed it. The war would have been over there and then if the marshes and woods had not given the fugitives cover.

'The army was emboldened by the victory, whether they knew about it first hand or from reports; nothing, they said, could resist them: they must forge ahead into Scotland and never stop fighting till they had found the very end of Britain. Even the men who had advised a prudent retreat the day before were now eager and boastful. This is the most unjust thing of all in war – everyone claims the credit for victory, but blames defeat on one man. For their part the British did not think they had been defeated through any failing of theirs, but by the good luck and skill of Agricola; with unabated doggedness they continued to arm their men, move their women and children to safety, and meet and sacrifice together to confirm their confederacy. Both sides departed for the winter with their enthusiasm at fever-pitch.'

Tacitus interrupts his narrative with an extraordinary story. Some German auxiliaries, stationed somewhere on the west coast of Britain, found that life in the Roman army, at least in this country, was more than they had bargained for:

'That same summer, a cohort of Usipi that had been conscripted in Germany and transferred to Britain committed a daring and remarkable crime. Their instructors were Roman soldiers, who had stayed with them as section commanders to keep them up to scratch. These, and the centurion, they now murdered, and boarded three warships after kidnapping the pilots. They became suspicious of two of these and killed them, but sailed away with the third to guide them before they were reported. It was an extraordinary exploit. Later they had to land for water and supplies; in their frequent skirmishes with the Britons defending their property they usually won; but being sometimes defeated they became so short of food that they ate the feeblest of their number; later they drew lots for their victims. They sailed right round Britain, but when their bad seamanship lost them their ships they were taken for pirates, and twice intercepted by Dutch and German tribes. Some were sold as slaves, and passed from owner to owner till they reached our bank of the Rhine, where their account of these great adventures made them notorious.'

At the beginning of AD 84 Agricola must have known that the following summer would be his last in Britain. He would have completed seven years in command, a length of office with few parallels in the empire. He determined that this year would bring him final success; he had another reason for losing himself in hard work, as well:

'At the beginning of the summer Agricola suffered a great personal blow in the death of his little son, born the year before. He did not bear this loss with a conventional, ostentatious courage, nor yet with womanly tears and wails. He found a cure for his grief in the war. He sent the fleet ahead to spread anxiety and terror by frequent raids. He added to the army some units from the bravest of the Britons, whose loyalty was proved by their long obedience. Marching light he reached the Graupian Mountain, and found it occupied by the enemy. They were in no way dismayed by their last defeat. They were looking forward to revenge: it was either that or slavery. At last they realised that a common danger demanded action in common: by sending round embassies and making treaties, they had called out the strength of all the states. There were already over 30,000 armed men to be seen, and still they were flowing in, not only young men, but even those whose "old age was fresh and green", war heroes, each with his decorations.'

Tacitus goes on to 'record' the speeches delivered by the opposing generals. Both are imaginary – Agricola even answers points in his opponent's speech as if they were debating. But Calgacus does at least list the grievances of the British, and there is no reason to suppose them untrue – conscription, slavery, taxation of corn and money, forced labour on road-building, all accompanied by blows and insults. And there is one memorable sentence:

'For robbery, murder and looting they use the lying word "empire", and when they have brought desolation, they call it peace.'

Another grim and bloody battle followed, and again, as in every set piece, discipline outweighed the superior numbers of the British. The auxiliary infantry and cavalry had all the fighting – the legions were not even called in. The cavalry mowed down every resistance, and pursued unmercifully. By nightfall some 10,000 Britons had been killed – Roman casualties numbered 360. We do not know where the Graupian Mountain is, but the line of marching camps from Inchtuthil to a point near the mouth of the Spey, where Agricola's most northerly camp was recognised in 1967, probably indicates the line of his march. His last battle could well have been in Inverness-shire or Morayshire. Tacitus vividly pictures the scene:

'By nightfall our men had won the reward for victory – satisfaction and booty. The British dispersed, men and women weeping together, dragging off their

110

wounded, and calling to the survivors. They left their homes, and in a senseless fury set them on fire, chose hiding-places and at once left them. They grouped to form some sort of plan, but then broke up. Sometimes the sight of their loved ones broke their hearts, more often it drove them to a frenzy. It was discovered that some of them, in a strange kind of pity, put their own wives and children to death.

'On the next day the shape of victory was easier to see. Everywhere was a great silence: the hills were deserted, in the distance smoke rose from their houses. Not a soul met our scouts – they had been sent in every direction to reconnoitre, and found only the traces of unorganised flight – the enemy was nowhere regrouping. Agricola, however, could not extend operations, for the summer was over; he led the army into the territory of the Boresti, who surrendered. He ordered the admiral of the fleet to sail round Britain. Forces were allotted for the task, and it was helped by its grim reputation, which preceded it. Agricola himself marched slowly back with the infantry and cavalry, to overawe fresh tribes by his deliberate progress, before placing them in winter quarters. And at the same time the fleet, with favourable winds, made its way back into the harbour of Trucculum, full of honour. This was the base from which it had surveyed the neighbouring coast.'

This reference to the fleet is perplexing. There would not have been nearly enough time to sail right round Britain while the army was marching – no matter how slowly – from Inverness to Inchtuthil. Dio Cassius tells us that the exploit of the Usipi prompted Agricola to order the circumnavigation. Since Roman ships had already sailed round all our shores south of the Clyde and Forth, the truth may be that he merely wanted to complete the job by confirming that there *was* a passage round the north of the island. Earlier in the *Agricola* Tacitus mentioned the voyage, and added . . . 'the fleet . . . at the same time discovered and subdued some islands previously unknown, called the Orkneys'. With good weather – which the fleet had – it might have been possible to sail by John O'Groats and Cape Wrath down into The Minch, back into the Orkneys and down to the Tay, before the winter storms.

Agricola's report of his success was greeted with acclaim in Rome. He was recalled and granted triumphal regalia, a splendid statue, and everything short of the full triumph that was reserved for the emperor and his family. Tacitus alleges that the emperor Domitian was jealous, or scared, of this popularity. True or not, Agricola was never employed again, but left to an inconspicuous retirement. He died in August AD 93.

14

Two Walls

When Agricola left Britain in AD 84, Tacitus' interest in the island came to an end, and for the next 100 years other ancient authors have very little to say. But a number of inscriptions and a great deal of work by archaeologists in recent years have gone a long way to make sense out of the few scanty references we have.

In AD 85 the Roman empire was threatened by a tough people called the Dacians living north of the Danube. Troops were urgently needed, and soon afterwards the Second Support Legion was recalled from Britain. The great number of Agricola's forts in Scotland had already stretched the troops pretty thin. With the army now reduced to three legions and a corresponding number of auxiliaries, there was no longer any hope that the frontier could be carried right to the northern shores of Scotland, and retreat was necessary.

The Twentieth Legion was moved from the fortress at Inchtuthil to replace the Second Support Legion at Chester; the move was not intended to be permanent. In 1958 excavators uncovered *seven tons* of nails, large and small, that the Roman soldiers had buried at Inchtuthil to keep them out of enemy hands; if they had not meant to return they would have taken this valuable supply with them, for their retreat was orderly and planned, not a hurried evacuation.

The frontier was pulled back to the Clyde–Forth line of forts established by Agricola, and the forts in the Lowlands reorganised. The fort at Newstead, for example, was increased from ten to 14 acres, and its rampart doubled – it was now 45 feet thick. Excavations have shown that a number of the Lowlands forts were rebuilt in a burst of activity at this time.

Tacitus has only one wry comment to make; in a summary of the period he wrote:

'The Balkans were in an uproar, the loyalty of the Gallic provinces was faltering, and Britain was allowed to slip away the moment the conquest was complete.'

This is of course a gross exaggeration, but it may perhaps be forgiven. To Agricola, and inevitably to Tacitus, it seemed that seven years' hard work was being wasted. But in truth there was nothing else that Domitian could have done.

Trajan's column in Rome

In AD 101 the new emperor, Trajan, was again faced with trouble from the Dacians, and in two great campaigns he defeated them and brought them into the empire in a huge new province north of the Danube. 'Trajan's Column' was set up to celebrate his victory. On it the story of the campaigns is told in a series of sculptured pictures – rather like a strip cartoon – spiralling round the column; they are an invaluable source of information about the Roman army of the time, and its methods. (A plaster cast of Trajan's column can be seen in London at the Victoria and Albert Museum.)

Whether Trajan called for reinforcements from the British armies is not known, but soon, around the turn of the century, the army was pulled further back to the first line of the Agricolan forts along the Stanegate. Moreover, at some time after AD 100 a decision had been taken that the legionary fortresses at Caerleon, Chester and York should be made permanent. Timber was replaced by stone, and inscriptions have been found commemorating this reconstruction.

It is obvious that Trajan was content to let matters in Scotland rest as they were. He spent the next ten years or so on grandiose schemes, creating huge new provinces in Armenia, Mesopotamia and Assyria.

The emperor Hadrian

Scotland must have seemed very unimportant in comparison. But when he died in AD 117, his successor, Hadrian, saw that the resources of the empire had been strained too far, and that the frontiers of the empire would have to be redrawn.

In the fourth century a collection was made of the biographies of 30 emperors, written by several authors. The *Historia Augusta,* as the collection is called, is often dull and untrustworthy, but obviously important when other evidence is missing. The collection starts with Hadrian, and after describing Trajan's death recounts the events of AD 117:

'As soon as he gained power as emperor Hadrian immediately resumed the policy of the first emperors and devoted all his energies to maintaining world peace. For the nations subdued by Trajan began to revolt; in addition the Moors started making raids, and the Sarmatians full-scale war, while the Britons could not be kept under control; Egypt was torn by dissension, and Libya and Palestine made no secret of their intent to rebel. As a result Hadrian surrendered everything east of the Tigris and Euphrates. He used to say that he was following the example of Cato, who declared the Macedonians free because they could not be kept in subjection.'

This reference to trouble in Britain is confirmed by other evidence. As urgent reinforcements were needed in the province, the Sixth Legion sailed from Germany straight to the Tyne. In thanks for their safe arrival they dedicated two altar tablets to the gods of the sea by the simplest expedient – pitching them overboard: they were found in the mud when the new Swing Bridge over the Tyne was being made. They read simply:

'To Neptune (and To Ocean . . .) the Sixth Legion, Victorious, Loyal and True, (dedicates this.)'

Again, about 40 miles from Rome itself a tombstone of a veteran soldier was found; his career was described in full – at one time he was 'commanding officer of three detachments of 1,000 men from the Seventh, Eighth and Twenty Second Legions on the British Expedition.'

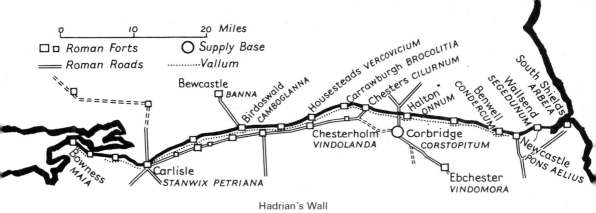

Hadrian's Wall

Why were such great and rapid reinforcements needed? It seems that the Ninth Legion, based at York, had suffered some shameful defeat, probably at the hands of the Brigantes, and was disbanded in disgrace, for from this time the Ninth Legion disappears from history, and the number was never used again. The Sixth, which replaced it, stayed in Britain with the Second Augustan and the Twentieth for nearly 300 years.

Though this rebellion was crushed by the following year, in AD 121 Hadrian came to Britain during a tour of the western provinces. In Germany he had found the army slack and inefficient, and worked hard to restore discipline: to encourage the men by his own example he joined them on 20-mile route marches wearing full armour, and 'cheerfully shared the soldiers' rations of bacon, cheese and vinegar'. The fate of the Ninth will have encouraged him to similar disciplinary action in Britain. But he saw that far more decisive measures were necessary, and that the troublesome Brigantes and their powerful neighbours to the north, the Selgovae, must be denied any chance of co-operation in the future. His biographer records:

'And so, having reformed his soldiers in princely fashion, he came to Britain and put right many things that were wrong. He was the first to build a wall, 80 miles long, to keep the barbarians and Romans apart.'

Hadrian's wall is an amazing and massive structure, one of the great achievements of the empire. Most of it was built between AD 122 and 128, but the details of it were changed several times while it was still under construction. It was between eight and ten feet thick, and 15 feet high. Troops could walk along it, protected by a parapet another five or six feet high. At first the western half from the river Irthing was made of turf, as stone was scarce in this region, but before long stone was carried across and used for all its length.

Along it are 79 mile castles, each a Roman mile (1,620 yards) apart, with a gate in the wall, leading out to the north; these fortlets were big enough for

VALLUM

|←—27'—→|←—20'—→|10'|←— — — — — Varies up to c. 1000ˣ — — — —→|←—20'—→|←—30'— — —→|←—20'—→|←—30'— —→|←—20'—→|

WALL

Ditch about
13'6" deep

MILITARY
ROAD

8'
Ditch about
10'deep

Mound
6' high

Typical section through Hadrian's Wall

detachments of up to 50 men. Two small signal turrets, some 550 yards apart, were set between each pair of milecastles. Built into the wall at roughly equal intervals are 16 large forts, intended for infantry cohorts of 1,000 men, or cavalry *alae* of 500. About 9,500 men were deployed along the whole wall, all of them auxiliaries.

In front of the wall itself was a ditch, except where the cliffs made this impossible or unnecessary. In the central section the wall was built at the top of the steep slopes of the Whin Sill. A military road ran behind the wall, linking the forts, and south of that again another ditch, known as the *Vallum*. This formed the official limit of the southern side of the military zone, for the purpose of the whole wall system was political as well as military. It was not a defensive structure like a city wall. It controlled the movements of the unsettled British tribes to north and south, and allowed patrols to observe what was happening. Signals could swiftly be flashed along the wall, and from the wide doors in every fort and milecastle cavalry and infantry could dash out to deal with any sort of trouble.

Men of the Roman army garrisoned the wall for most of the next 300 years. Their wives and children lived and died in the civil settlements that grew up outside the walls of the forts. You can still see where the men kept guard, and slept, or joked and relaxed in the bath-houses. At Housesteads, newly cleared of earth, is one of their latrines, with smart gullies and basins; here they washed their hands and the sponges they used instead of toilet paper.

Part of the Wall today

At Corbridge, in a small wooden hut, is a magnificent collection of objects that recall the busy life of workmen and soldiers – chisels and hammers, drills and files, spear-heads and armour, sling-bullets and handcuffs. There are even the cooking pots of the housewives, a child's tea set, an infant's feeding bottle (they used leather teats – most unhygienic!), a draughts board and pieces.

But the wall, great though it was, soon became outdated. When Hadrian died in AD 138 the new emperor, Antoninus, quickly changed frontier policy. Roman troops again moved forward into the Lowlands and built a new barrier, this time on the line of Agricola's forts between the Clyde and Forth. The *Historia* records of Antoninus:

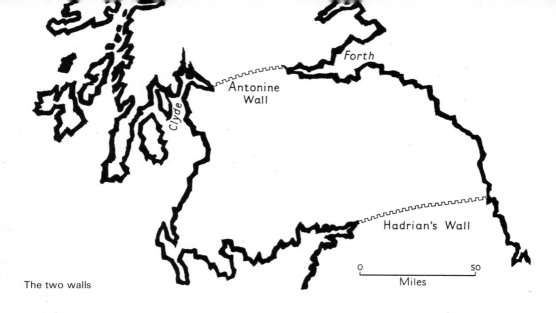

The two walls

'Acting through his legates he fought a number of wars; for he had Lollius Urbicus, the governor, conquer the Britons, drive off the barbarians, and build another wall, of turf.'

This wall, still visible in many places, was 37 miles long. In front of it was a ditch, 40 feet wide and 12 feet deep, and behind it a military road. On a stone foundation 14 feet wide stood a wall of turf some nine feet high, topped with a wooden breastwork, adding perhaps another five feet. Roughly every two miles there was a fort – the biggest at Mumrills covered over seven acres, the smallest at Duntocher only just over half an acre. The military road linked the forts, and most of these had annexes which came to be used by civilian traders and hangers-on. The whole system is much simpler than Hadrian's Wall; fewer troops and less money were needed.

Hadrian's Wall was abandoned: earth from the mounds was thrown into the Vallum ditch to make causeways, and the gates of the milecastles were removed. A few troops were left in the forts for routine maintenance duties.

We cannot say for certain why the new wall was built at all: perhaps it was a combination of Antoninus' ambition and the need to suppress troublesome tribes north of the old wall. A Greek historian of the time, Pausanias, wrote:

'Antoninus never made war of his own accord, but when the Moors took up arms against Rome, he drove them out of all their lands . . . he also took most of their territory away from the Brigantes because they too had invaded Genunia, which is subject to Rome.'

118

This statement is not very helpful, because we do not know where Genunia was, nor why Pausanias should mention the Brigantes as if they were outside the province, when they had already been firmly in it for over 60 years. Perhaps he uses the name carelessly, and really means their allies the Selgovae, who may have been trying to re-establish contact with them after being separated by Hadrian's wall.

In AD 155 there was more trouble. Some of Antoninus' coins for that year show a subdued Britannia – rather like the figure on the reverse of a penny – which probably indicates the successful end of fighting somewhere in the country. A stone dredged from the Tyne has this inscription:

'To the Emperor Antoninus Augustus Pius, Father of his Country, the reinforcements for the Second Augustan Legion, the Second Legion Victorious, and the Twentieth Valerian Legion from the Two German Provinces, under Julius Verus, Governor of Britain, (set up this stone).'

Archaeologists have shown that the forts of the Antonine wall were evacuated and burnt, and that soon afterwards the gates of the milecastles in Hadrian's wall were re-hung, and the Vallum cleared again.

On the death of Antoninus in AD 161 Marcus Aurelius became emperor, and the *Historia Augusta* records at the beginning of his reign that a certain Calpurnius Agricola was sent to deal with a war threatening in Britain; more inscriptions indicate that some forts in north Britain were rebuilt during his period as governor. By this time too the forts of the Antonine wall had been restored.

But for the next 25 years our sources are silent, and it is reasonable to presume that the troops on the two walls met with little trouble, and that the southern section of Scotland, as well as the north of England, learnt to accept, perhaps even to value, a Roman peace.

15

Town . . .

The Romans occupied Britain to enlarge and strengthen their empire. They also hoped after the conquest to increase their trade by finding new markets for their goods and fresh sources of minerals and foodstuffs. And they had no doubt that to spread the Roman way of life to less civilised peoples was in itself an act of kindness.

None of these peaceful ambitions could be fulfilled without an efficient system of local and national government, supported by just laws, and paid for by regular taxes. Market places, law courts and tax offices were the essential ingredients. Where were they to be found? The Roman mind saw but one answer – in the towns which were so numerous all over the rest of the empire, but so completely absent in Britain. Where no towns existed, they would have to be built.

London may have looked like this in the 1st Century AD

1 Venta Icenorum
2 Camulodunum
3 Verulamium
4 Londinium
5 Eburacum
6 Lindum Colonia
7 Ratae
8 Calleva
9 Noviomagus
10 Durovernum
   Cantiacorum
11 Deva
12 Viroconium
13 Venta Silurum
14 Isca Dumnoniorum
15 Durnovaria
16 Corinium
   Dobunnorum
17 Petuaria
18 Glevum

The towns and peoples of Britain

Six years after the invasion, as we saw, a colony of veterans was founded at Colchester. A *colonia* was a town with a charter, principally for Roman citizens. In this town each veteran was given a plot for his house, while outside the town he had land to farm. Also, of course, room was found for the Trinovantes in whose territory the colony was built – in fact it became their tribal capital.

Not far away was Verulamium, near modern St. Albans, the capital of the Catuvellauni. Tacitus tells us that it was a *municipium*, a self-governing borough. As Boudicca's warriors burnt it to the ground, it seems that its inhabitants must have adopted Roman ways so thoroughly that the rebels treated them as cruelly as the Romans.

Soon to become more important and larger than these two was London. Probably given the status of *colonia* or *municipium*, it became the financial and administrative capital of the whole province. Some idea of the speed of development emerged from Tacitus' account of the Boudicca rebellion. Colchester had a senate house, a temple and a theatre, as well as private houses, even though all these were built of wood and burnt to the ground. London and Verulamium may not have been as impressive to look at, but at least they were large enough to hold many thousands of Romans – even if Tacitus exaggerated when he told of 70,000 slain.

After the destruction, rebuilding went on apace. Classicianus and the governors who followed the revengeful Suetonius were successful in their efforts to pacify and romanise the province. Tacitus gives the credit to Agricola for encouraging the Britons to build their towns and adopt the Roman way of life. But a fragment of stone from the gable of some building at the health resort of Bath reads 'Vespasian, consul for the seventh time' – the date is AD 76. In 1955 an inscription was discovered at Verulamium from the massive gateway of the forum. It dates the building exactly to the second half of AD 79 – and this too must have been begun before Agricola arrived as governor.

Soon there were four colonies, all originating from great army bases: Colchester, founded in AD 49, was followed by Lincoln (LINdum COLoNia) and Gloucester. These were towns which succeeded legionary fortresses when the legions moved on, but at York the colony and fortress grew up side by side. A good deal of the country around these four colonies was given to them, and came under their control.

There was one class of towns that the Romans were particularly anxious should be built quickly and handsomely. These were the capitals of the most influential tribes in the province. In the past the various tribes had been fiercely independent, caring only for themselves and their farmsteads. But when they saw magnificent towns, with great public buildings, rising from the fields, they could at last understand the superiority of the power which now controlled the country. As traffic increased along the highroads they would see that their tribe was but one small part of a large and united country. We can imagine the pride of the local aristocrats as they learnt to live in these fine centres, and from them to govern their people.

Tacitus gives us an inkling of the story in his account of Agricola's activities:

'The following year (AD 79–80) was devoted to the most sensible policies. A people which is scattered and uncivilised is quick to fight. To make peace and leisure acceptable he had to show how pleasant they were, so he gave to both individuals and communities encouragement and official assistance to build temples, town-centres and houses, with praise for co-operation and rebuke for all who were reluctant. They competed to win his favour, and compulsion was unnecessary. He went further, and made sure that the sons of the chieftains received a proper education. He declared that the intelligence of the Britons was worth more than the careful learning of the Gauls: the result was that men who had a short time before refused to learn Latin were now anxious to speak it fluently. Then too Roman fashions were popular, and the toga was to be seen everywhere. Gradually the Britons sank to the demoralising pleasures to be found in the porticoes, bath-houses and elegant dinner-parties. These simple people called it "civilisation": really it was only one way of keeping them quiet.'

This is a cynical view with which few Romans or Britons would have agreed.

We know of 14 tribal capitals: here is a list of them. Most of their names are double-barrelled; the town-name is followed by the name of the tribe, in the genitive case. For example, *Corinium Dobunnorum* means 'Corinium, capital of the Dobunni'.

Isurium Brigantum	Aldborough	Yorkshire
Petuaria (Parisi)	Brough	Yorkshire
Viroconium Cornoviorum	Wroxeter	Shropshire
Venta Icenorum	Caistor St. Edmunds	Norfolk
Ratae Coritanorum	Leicester	
Verulamium (Catuvellauni)	St. Albans	Hertfordshire
Corinium Dobunnorum	Cirencester	Gloucestershire
Venta Silurum	Caerwent	Monmouthshire
Calleva Atrebatum	Silchester	Hampshire
Durovernum Cantiacorum	Canterbury	Kent
Venta Belgarum	Winchester	Hampshire
Noviomagus Regnensium	Chichester	Sussex
Isca Dumnoniorum	Exeter	Devon
Durnovaria (Durotriges)	Dorchester	Dorset

The official assistance which Agricola gave to the tribal leaders was not only in the form of money. The legions lent them surveyors, architects and craftsmen; it is not surprising that the public buildings of these tribal towns are very similar to the main structures of the legionary fortresses.

In the centre of the town was the *forum* – the word translated as 'town-centre'. The plan of some of the town-centres has been discovered by excavation, but one town has revealed almost its whole lay-out. For Silchester,

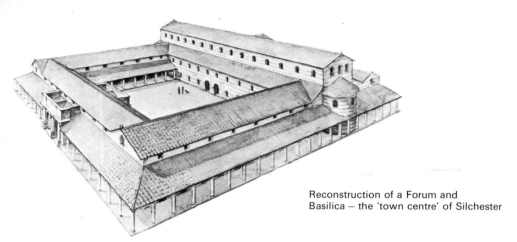

Reconstruction of a Forum and
Basilica — the 'town centre' of Silchester

near Reading, became a dead town even in Roman times, and was never built over. It was carefully investigated in a great series of excavations at the end of last century. In Mr. G. C. Boon's book *Roman Silchester,* to accompany the plan and imaginary reconstruction of the forum is this description:

'The Forum, or market-place, consists of a large open court surrounded by porticoes, shops and offices on three sides, and on the fourth and west by the Basilica or town hall – a great hall much larger than the Guildhall of London, flanked by a row of spacious offices including the *curia* or council chamber of the tribe. The whole is surrounded by an outer portico. Throughout, the work was of the best construction, with walls from 3 to 4 feet thick of dressed courses of flints with tile quoins and bonds. The east wall of the Basilica was 5 feet thick, to sustain the tremendous weight of that part of the building. The roof was partly tiled and partly of the hexagonal Old Red Sandstone or Pennant Grit slabs familiar in the villa regions of the west country. The ranges of the Forum probably stood about 45 feet high, and the Basilica about 70 feet high.'

The council which met in the *curia* was called an *ordo:* it was composed of 100 of the richest citizens, called *decurions.* Every year they elected from their number four magistrates, two to look after legal matters, and two, equivalent to borough engineer and surveyor, who cared for the public buildings, markets and streets. At the end of their year of office these magistrates were granted Roman citizenship. They presided in the local courts, judging all but the most important cases, and collected the taxes imposed by the central government in London as well as the local rates for the upkeep of the town amenities.

Round the forum was a grid of streets, which divided the town into rectangular areas known as *insulae,* islands. In these were the public buildings

124

Silchester from the air

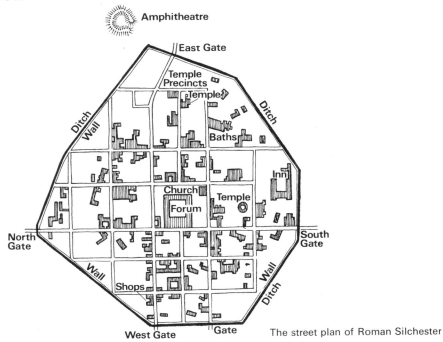

Amphitheatre

East Gate

Temple
Precincts

Temple

Ditch

Baths

Ditch

Wall

Inn

Church

Forum

Temple

North
Gate

South
Gate

Wall

Ditch

Wall

Shops

West Gate

Gate

The street plan of Roman Silchester

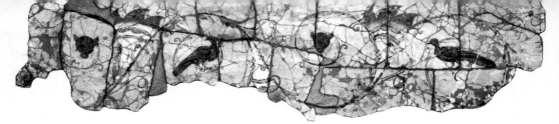

like the *mansio* – a guest house for travelling officials – and the public baths, and private houses and shops.

At first the houses were long narrow buildings with four or five rooms, with the narrow gabled end on the street. The walls were often made of the simplest materials: clay was daubed onto interlaced wooden strips, and the surface was then smoothed and painted. Some large fragments of this form of wall and decoration can be seen in the Verulam Museum at St. Albans.

Later houses were often larger and built in a square around an open court-yard. Plaster replaced the clay daub, and walls and ceilings were elaborately painted. Mosaic floors were laid – small pieces of coloured stone and marble arranged in patterns and pictures upon a concrete base.

During the second century an under-floor central heating system, known as a hypocaust, was introduced into the richer houses. The floor was sup-ported on pillars, and hot air and smoke from a furnace room circulated in the empty spaces and through flues in the walls to the air above.

Bath-houses were large, and constantly being altered through the years. They were like modern Turkish baths. At Silchester the bather exercised or played one of several ball-games in an exercise yard *(palaestra)*. He then removed his clothes in an undressing-room *(apodyterium)* and walked through an unheated room with a plungebath of cold water *(frigidarium)* to the first heated room *(tepidarium)*. Here he began to sweat, a process completed in the very hot sweat-room *(sudatorium)*. He probably spent some time in a hot room *(calidarium)*, where he rubbed in olive oil (used instead of soap) and scraped off the mixture of sweat, dirt and oil with a scraper of metal or bone called a *strigil*.

Then, after a dip in the hot bath, he returned to the cold room for a cold

A hypocaust

A mosaic floor from Verulamium

An aerial view of the theatre at Verulamium

bath or shower. Off the undressing room was the massage and anointing room *(unctorium)*, for the last stage in the ritual before dressing. One wonders how many were tempted by the English climate to miss out the cold shower!

Public entertainment was provided in the amphitheatre, which was usually set apart from the town, and outside the walls which were built in the third century. The magistrates were expected to put on some of the shows, which might include bull fights, bear-baiting, cockfighting or any of the gruesome and bloody contests the Romans loved. Boxing, wrestling and circus shows were other possibilities, but there was very little of the theatrical drama we might expect. There were, so far as we know, only four theatres in Britain – and these were probably used for religious masques and ceremonies rather than for the production of plays.

Only London, the four colonies, and the tribal capitals had the large imposing town-centres. These were obviously intended for government purposes, whether national or local. The Ordnance Survey Map of Roman Britain lists 23 smaller walled towns, two spas at Buxton and Bath, and no less than 53 other major settlements. And all of these, with perhaps only one or two exceptions, were inspired and founded by the Romans, who brought with them a way of life that has, to some degree, lasted until today.

16

These discarded
wine-barrels
were use to
line a Roman
well at Silchester

. . . and Country

The new towns, and the roads which linked them together, changed the face of Britain for ever. They are the first and most visible sign of romanisation. But the countryside also saw changes, though here they came less quickly and less obviously.

Most of the Celtic inhabitants of the country were farmers of one sort or another, growing corn or herding sheep and cattle, and efficiently, too. Strabo told us that even before the occupation corn and hides were exported to the continent. But with the coming of the Romans, for various reasons farming flourished as never before.

In the first place, the new towns provided a sure and growing market. The more enterprising Britons cut down – and probably sold – their timber, and planted more corn or bred more sheep or cattle, in the rich fertile land now being profitably used for the first time.

Secondly, though the Romans brought no new agricultural methods with them, they did introduce superior techniques which helped production. Wells, for instance, were dug deeply and safely. With improved ploughs, and better drainage, more land could be developed. Corn was now artificially dried in a special oven; the result was healthier grain that could be kept from one year to the next with far less wastage. And the new roads promoted a quicker and safer exchange of produce.

Third, the army quartermasters were insatiable. Meat and wool and leather were in constant demand, and many Britons must have made their fortunes out of the army of occupation. But for the supply of corn there was no payment. This was a tax on the British farmers, and one that caused considerable hardship, as we have seen. As much as half of the crop had to be transported, without recompense, to the army camps and fortresses.

The over-all result, though, whether the produce was profitable or not, was that in the lowland region of the country, roughly the land to the south and east of the Fosse Way, agriculture prospered.

Most of the farmsteads in Britain were of the type found at Little Woodbury – round, timber-framed and thatched – and most of them changed very little throughout the whole period of Roman occupation. Their owners, however, did use the new designs of pottery, and the improved tools imported by the Romans; they also planted some of the new fruits and crops, such as

E

A reconstruction of the villa at Lockleys

apple, plum and cherry, flax, rye, carrots and cabbage.

But some of the farmers living near the new towns, or along the high roads, had the commercial sense to exploit their advantageous position. With their new wealth they built a different type of farmhouse; these romanised farmhouses are called *villas*. However, it is important to remember that though the buildings were of a Roman type, the occupants were Britons, not Romans. They were not the lowest peasant class, for they had plenty of money to spend. Nor were they the local aristocrats of the *curia*, for these tribal leaders had been warriors and landowners, not farmers. They had built the towns with Agricola's help and encouragement, and lived in them, in houses larger and more sophisticated than the villas, even though these were a great improvement on the native huts they replaced. The villa occupants may have been an independent middle-class, or tenants or agents of the aristocrats. There are, it is true, some 70 very large and luxurious villas, quite grand enough for the local aristocrats; but these were not built until much later, most of them in the fourth century.

A typical example of villa development is to be found near St. Albans at a site called Lockleys. Here excavations have revealed that the first building was a circular hut, some four yards across. This was succeeded by a larger hut, whose occupants replaced their broken crocks with Roman pottery. Then, about AD 70, the house was completely rebuilt. The new plan was a rectangle; there were five rooms, and a verandah, supported by a row of posts. The lower parts of the walls were made of flint and mortar on a foundation of chalk and flint. The upper part of the wall was covered in plaster, and this was painted. The floors were tiled. Villas of this type have been found all over north Europe.

Then, towards the end of the second century, the house was rebuilt again,

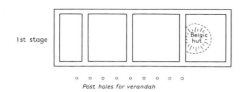

1st stage

Belgic hut

Post holes for verandah

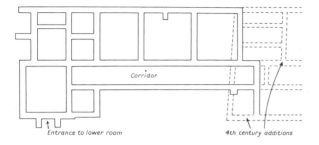

Corridor

Entrance to lower room

4th century additions

Plan of
Lockleys villa

and greatly enlarged. The verandah was superseded by a corridor, and a wing was added at each end. This pattern of building is common enough to have a special name; it is known as a 'winged corridor' villa. One of these wings had two storeys, the lower one some five feet below the level of the rest of the villa.

For all its new elegance, the villa was still a farmhouse, accompanied by barns, stables, pig-sties and so on; and this is generally true of all the villas. They are a working part of the agricultural system.

The development at Lockleys, and at many other sites – around 600 villa sites are known in this country – reflects the growing prosperity of the province and the empire in general. Villas were built not only as working farmhouses, but to give pleasure as well. Lucius Columella, in a treatise written around the time the first villa was built at Lockleys, after describing a suitable farmhouse, goes on:

'The master should build the best possible house that is compatible with his financial resources, so that it may entice him not only to come to the country more willingly, but also to stay in it with greater pleasure. Especially is this the case if he is accompanied by his wife. Her feelings, like those of all her sex, are more fastidious, and she will have to be humoured by some comfortable features to induce her to stay more happily with her husband. Let the farmer build elegantly, therefore.'

The *Ordnance Survey Map of Roman Britain* shows that nearly all the villas are in the south-east of the country. This was the richest part of the province, and the part most influenced by Roman ways. Moreover, it can be seen how the villas are grouped round the towns and along the main roads and track-

Sheep shears

ways; this was essential if the produce was to get to market.

On the other hand, there are very few villas around the colonies. When the veterans were settled here, they were given a plot of land in the town itself, and though their livelihood depended on the acres for cultivation which they were allotted in the surrounding countryside, they were expected to build a house and to live in the town. The lack of villas round a few other towns, like London, Silchester and Canterbury, seems to indicate a similar arrangement, but we do not know the reason for it.

There are two other special areas in lowland Britain where there are virtually no villas or towns, but a great number of farms of the native type. The first is to the north and west of Salisbury, nearly 1,000 square miles in extent; the other, over twice as large, is the Fenland around the Wash. It is believed that these were Imperial estates, owned by the Roman government. On them corn was grown, either for the army, or to be exported as a profitable venture.

The Romans were the first people to drain the Fens and make them habitable, when a slight change in the level of the land gave the chance of occupation. The most notable drainage work is the Car Dyke, a canal running from the Fens to Lincoln. It also provided a means of transport; barges carrying corn could pass along it to Lincoln, then westward by the Foss Dyke to the Trent, and up this river and the Ouse right to the great army base at York, and return laden with coal. Salt was another important product of this area.

But agriculture was not the only industry of the countryside. The Romans had come for minerals as well. The tin trade, for which Britain was first known, had declined at the time of the invasion; an alternative source had been found in Spain. Only one gold mine was discovered, but this was important enough to justify the construction of an aqueduct over six miles long, bringing water to wash the ore. The shafts underground were drained by water wheels; a similar water wheel, from a mine in Spain, can be seen in the British Museum in London.

In his *Natural History*, Pliny records:

'Lead is used for the manufacture of pipes and thin sheets. In Spain and Gaul it is mined with difficulty, but in Britain there are such large quantities near the surface that there is a law limiting its exploitation.'

The first lead mines were in the Mendips in Somerset, and two ingots from this area carry an inscription dating them to AD 49. Perhaps more important than the lead itself was the silver that could be extracted from it, by a process known as cupellation. Initially the mines were managed as state concerns, but were later leased to private companies; this may be due to the fact that the percentage of silver in British lead was much lower than that to be found

A table leg
made of shale

in other parts of the empire. Copper was mined in Shropshire and Wales: it was mainly used with zinc, lead or tin in alloys of brass or bronze.

The commonest metal was iron, and its ore was worked in many parts of the country, though the most productive areas were the Weald of Kent and east Sussex, Gloucestershire and Lincolnshire. Iron tools were used everywhere, mostly locally made; the traces of a great number of simple furnaces have been noted. The army was perhaps the largest consumer.

In the north and west of the province coal was obviously a popular fuel. It was not mined, but quarried from surface veins, which were numerous enough to make mining unnecessary. Large quantities have been found, bunkered ready for use, in some of the forts along Hadrian's Wall. And enough has been found in the south and east of England to show that supplies were distributed all over the country.

Stone quarries produced millstones and whetstones as well as building stone. At Kimmeridge, in Dorset, a soft, soapy, stone known as shale was quarried, and worked into decorative table legs, trays, couch-frames and even drinking cups. Whetstones from a quarry near Stony Stratford have been discovered as far afield as London and Norwich. A rich, black stone called jet, which can be highly polished, came from Whitby in Yorkshire, and rings, necklaces and decorative jewellery were made from it. Ready-made articles are exported, and a number have been unearthed in Germany. When a piece of jet is rubbed briskly, it will, like amber, attract small pieces of paper or fluff, and this 'magic' must have increased its value.

Pearls, hunting dogs, oysters, leather, timber and window-glass – the list goes on. Life in the countryside was as busy and varied as in the towns, and here too Roman influences were no less dominating.

17

Mutiny and Disaster

Trajan, Hadrian, Antoninus, Marcus Aurelius: these four men guided the empire to its greatest splendour. It was no chance that brought them to the throne. It had become the practice for the emperor, with the title of Augustus, to choose carefully a younger, able man, with the title of Caesar, as a colleague. On the death of the Augustus the Caesar took over his position and title, and then chose his own Caesar, and so on. But Marcus Aurelius' choice was disastrous. When his son Commodus succeeded in AD 180, he was more interested in chariot racing and riotous living, and left government largely in the hands of his ministers.

In the year AD 184 Cassius Dio records that Commodus was engaged in several wars:

'But the most serious was the one in Britain. The tribes in the island crossed the wall which separated them from the Roman legions, and while causing considerable damage cut down a general at the head of his troops. In some alarm Commodus sent Ulpius Marcellus to deal with them. He was a moderate and thrifty man, and when on active service always lived like an ordinary soldier in every respect, even eating the same rations; yet he was becoming haughty and arrogant. He was ostentatiously honest, but hard-hearted and stern.

'He needed less sleep than any other general; since he wanted the other officers to be equally on the alert, on most evenings he wrote twelve order-tablets . . . and had an adjutant deliver them to his various officers at different times, so that they might think their general was awake, and accordingly reduce their own sleeping time. He was, in the first place, by nature able to resist sleep, an ability he encouraged by fasting. He cut down on most foods, and in particular had his bread sent from Rome, to avoid eating his fill even of that. He did this not because he could not eat the local bread, but so that his bread should be so stale that he wouldn't eat a mouthful more than was absolutely necessary – his gums were tender, and dry bread made them bleed. At any rate, he wanted to appear to need less sleep than anyone else, so he deliberately exaggerated this natural ability.

'This was the type of man Marcellus was; he wrought terrible havoc on the barbarians in Britain.'

It was the Antonine wall which the barbarians crossed and destroyed. When Marcellus had crushed the invaders, he did not bother to repair it, and the wall was abandoned. For it had done its work. In the 40 odd years of its existence the lowlanders had learnt to prefer Roman rule; they acted as a buffer state between Hadrian's wall and the less civilised northerners. The trouble which now confronted Rome came not from the British, but from mutiny in the legions.

Marcellus cannot have been an easy man to serve under. Disgruntled and rebellious, the soldiers tried to persuade one of the lieutenants to seize Commodus' throne. When he refused, the soldiers looked for a scapegoat to excuse their behaviour. Disgusted at some promotions made by Commodus' chief minister, Perennis, they sent 1,500 men to Rome to complain. They met Commodus outside the city; he chose to accept their story. Here is the account of the *Historia Augusta*:

'At this time Perennis was claiming that the successes in Sarmatia of the other generals had been won by his son. This Perennis was a very powerful man; however, in the British war, he had deposed senatorial commanders and replaced them with men of equestrian rank; when a delegation from the army reported this, he was suddenly declared an outlaw, and handed over to the soldiers *to be torn to pieces.*'

Another passage continues the story:

'After Perennis' death, Commodus made up with Pertinax, and sent him a letter asking him to set out for Britain. He went, and stamped out every sign of mutiny, even though they wanted a change of emperor, preferably Pertinax himself . . . A rebellion against himself in Britain he suppressed at considerable personal risk; for when a legion mutinied he was almost killed, and left for dead. Pertinax took ruthless vengeance. In the end he asked to be excused from his governorship, saying the legions hated him for his strict discipline.'

Six years later, after Commodus' assassination in AD 193, Pertinax did become emperor. But his strictness was no less unpopular, and within three months he was killed. Then the throne was put up for auction by the troops, and knocked down to an old senator called Julian; but he too only lasted three months.

Three men then made a bid for supreme power – Pescennius Niger in

Septimius Severus

Syria, Clodius Albinus, governor of Britain, and Septimius Severus, who had won the support of the 16 legions on the Rhine and Danube. Severus reached Rome first and had himself declared Augustus. He won over Albinus by giving him the title of Caesar, and then annihilated Pescennius. But within a year he could no longer tolerate Albinus' position. He not only wanted the succession for his sons, but also suspected Albinus' popularity with the senate, which the *Historia Augusta* accounts for in these words:

'I do not think it irrelevant to explain how Albinus won the senate's regard. Commodus had ordered him to take command of the army in Britain, and offered him the title of Caesar – then news came that Commodus had died, though this was not yet true. Albinus went to the troops and spoke as follows: ' "If the Senate of the Roman people retained its former powers and the mighty empire were not in the hands of a single man, then men like Vitellius, Nero or Domitian would never have controlled the state. It was the Senate that added Africa to the Roman empire, the Senate conquered Gaul and Spain, brought law and order to the East, the Senate dared to attack the Parthians – and would have conquered them if Rome's ill-luck had not appointed such a greedy general to command the army (Crassus). Caesar was still a Senator when he conquered Britain, and not yet dictator. Commodus himself would have been a far better emperor if he had stood in awe of the Senate. The Senate still had influence and power even as late as the time of Nero, and wasn't afraid to criticise him and condemn him as a foul and disgusting emperor, even though he still held the throne with power of life and death. And so, fellow-soldiers, I refuse the title of Caesar which Commodus has offered me. May the gods grant that no-one else wants it. Let the Senate take over the empire, assign the provinces, and appoint us consuls . . ." '

So Severus resolved to be rid of Albinus, and tried treachery. By trusted couriers he sent Albinus a letter, begging him to share the throne, and calling him his 'most loyal, most dear and loving friend'.

'He told the couriers to hand over the letter in public, and then to say later that they had more matters to discuss in private, concerning the war, military secrets, and palace security. When they had come to the secret meeting, supposedly to report their instructions, five tough men were to murder him, with daggers concealed beneath their cloaks.

Clodius Albinus

'They did not let him down. They went to Albinus, and handed him the letter; when he had read it, they said they had matters to discuss more privately, and asked for a secluded place which no-one could overlook. But when they requested that Albinus should go to a distant portico completely alone, on the ground that their secrets might be betrayed, Albinus saw the danger of treachery. In the end he bowed to his suspicions, and had them tortured. For a long time in the beginning they denied everything, but eventually they were forced to confess Severus' instructions.'

Albinus realised that war was inevitable, and began to prepare. He would have to take all the troops from Britain with him to the continent – his only hope was to defeat Severus quickly and completely. But he also saw that the province would in some way have to be defended against the barbarians if he withdrew all the troops. He gave orders that an earth rampart and a ditch should be built round the towns – there was no time for proper walls of stone.

No literary source tells us when the first earthworks were put round most of Britain's towns, and archaeological evidence is as yet uncertain; Albinus' expedition to the continent provides the most likely circumstances.

In the autumn of AD 196 Albinus sailed to Gaul – the first occasion on which the continent was invaded from the island. There he had himself proclaimed Augustus, probably with the hope of encouraging the Gallic legions to join him.

'He collected a huge army, and advanced against Severus and his generals. In the first engagement he met the generals, and defeated them. Later Severus, compelling the Senate to declare Albinus a public enemy, set out himself and fought some brave and bitter battles in Gaul, with varying success. Finally, in some anxiety, he consulted fortune-tellers. They told him that Albinus would fall into his hands, neither living nor dead.

'And that is what happened. For when the final battle was joined, when countless of his men had been slaughtered, very many put to flight, and great numbers had surrendered, Albinus fled. Some reports allege that he stabbed himself, others that he was stabbed by his slave, and brought to Severus half dead. So the prophecy came true. But there were many reports that he was killed by his own soldiers, who, by killing him, tried to win Severus' favour.'

The Risingham inscription

By the time Albinus was defeated at Lyons in February, AD 197, the northerners in Britain had seized their chance. The tribes beyond the wall were grouped in two main confederacies, the Maeatae and the Caledonians; they swept south, burning, killing, destroying. Some of the Brigantes and Welsh joined in. Many of the forts on Hadrian's wall, and long stretches of the wall itself, were demolished. At milecastle 37 you can still see how the posts of the gate were levered out of a vertical position. The posts were not set upright when the milecastle was rebuilt; the gap was simply filled in.

Severus sent Virius Lupus to recover the province, and inscriptions of AD 197 record work started by him in Yorkshire and Westmorland. But his troops were the beaten and demoralised soldiers of Albinus; since Severus could not afford to send more, Lupus had to *bribe* the Maeatae to retire. Even then fighting against the Brigantes went on for several years, for the earliest repair on the wall itself cannot be dated before AD 205.

One of these inscriptions, from an outpost north of the wall at Risingham, is particularly fine; it records a repair done under the governor of the time, Senecio. The missing two lines at the beginning can be safely conjectured from other similar inscriptions.

'In honour of the Emperors Lucius Septimius Severus Pius Pertinax Arabicus
Adiabenicus Parthicus Maximus, three times Consul, Augustus, and Marcus
Aurelius Antoninus Pius, twice Consul, Augustus, and of Publius Septimius Geta,
the noble Caesar, this gate and the walls, fallen down in the passage of time,
were restored from ground level by order of the governor, His Honour Alfenius
Senecio, under the supervision of Oclatinus Adventus, Their Majesties'
procurator, by the First Cavalry Cohort of the Vangiones, under their tribune
Aemilius Salvius.'

This needs some explanation.

Severus has added *Pius* and *Pertinax* to his name to show his place in the
continuous line of emperors.

The next three of his names are titles taken from his victorious campaigns
in *Arabia, Adiabene* and *Parthia.*

Marcus Aurelius Antoninus Pius is his elder son, usually called Caracalla,
and these names were given him to connect him in people's minds with the
popular Antonine dynasty.

Since Caracalla was consul for the second time in AD 205, and for the
third time in AD 208, this inscription must have been made between these
dates.

The elder son is an Augustus, the younger son, *Geta,* is only a Caesar.

Geta's name has been defaced because Caracalla had him executed after
their father's death.

Fallen down in the passage of time is only a polite fiction; no-one was ever
going to dare to record that imperial property had been damaged by the
enemy.

The many inscriptions from this time, recording repair work over the next
25 years, show how severely the wall had been damaged. So much had to be
rebuilt that it is hardly surprising that historians writing a couple of hundred
years later thought that Severus, not Hadrian, was the originator of the
wall.

Senecio recovered the wall, but had not strength enough to push north
into Scotland to punish the invaders. So he wrote to the emperor to say that
the situation was still dangerous, and asking him either to send reinforcements, or to come himself at the head of an expedition. Though he was so
ill that he had to be carried in a litter – Dio says he had gout – in AD 208

140

Severus came, for he was both anxious for personal glory, and afraid that his sons were being corrupted by court life in Rome.

Severus and Caracalla did the fighting, Geta was left in charge of the province in the rear. Something of the importance of Britain can be judged from the fact that Severus and his sons spent *three years* in this distant province. Dio's description of the barbarians might supply the explanation:

'There are two very big tribes in Britain, the Caledonians and the Maeatae; the names of the others have been merged into these two. The Maeatae live near the cross-wall which cuts the island in two, and the Caledonians behind them. Both tribes live on wild and waterless mountains, or on desolate and marshy plains. They do not have walls or towns or farms; they live by grazing cattle, hunting, and picking fruit from the trees. Though there are inexhaustible supplies of fish, they never eat them. They live in huts, wearing neither clothes nor shoes, sharing their womenfolk, and rearing all their children in common.

'They have, for the most part, a democratic form of government: their favourite occupation is plundering, and for this reason they choose their boldest men to rule them. They fight with chariots, with small, fast horses, and their infantry is both quick to move and steady as a rock in defence. They have shields and short spears, which have bronze knobs on the butt-ends – they bang these on their shields to frighten their enemies – and they also have daggers.

'They can endure cold and hunger, and any kind of hardship. They hide in their marshes, and hold out for days with only their heads above water. In the woods they live on the bark or roots of trees; for emergencies they prepare a certain kind of food, and if they eat a piece of this the size of a bean, they feel neither hunger nor thirst.'

No wonder they were not easily beaten! After a brief description of Britain, Dio continues:

'Of this territory we possess just under half. So Severus, wishing to subdue all of it, invaded Caledonia, and met countless troubles in doing so – cutting down woods, levelling heights, filling in swamps and bridging rivers. But he never fought a proper battle, or saw the enemy drawn up in formation. They put out sheep and cattle on purpose for the soldiers to plunder, so that they would be lured on till they were exhausted. Our men suffered terribly in the water, and were attacked whenever they were scattered. Then, being unable to march, they were killed by their comrades to save them from capture, and casualties reached nearly 50,000.

'But Severus did not give up till he had almost reached the end of the island . . . And so, having been carried through most of the enemy country – he really was carried most of the way in a covered chair because of his weakness – he returned to the friendly part, and came to terms with the Britons on condition that they evacuated a large strip of land . . .

'When the islanders revolted again, he summoned the soldiers, ordered them to invade their territory once more, and to kill everyone they met. When this was being done, and the Caledonians joined the rebellion of the Maeatae, he was getting ready to make a personal expedition against them. While so engaged his illness carried him off on the fourth of February . . . His last words, addressed to his sons, were:
' "Stick together, spend your money on the troops, and let everyone else go hang." '

Severus died at York in AD 211. His ashes were taken to Rome.

The details of the campaigns are confused and scanty. Archaeological evidence is little better. But it does not seem that Severus intended to occupy Scotland permanently; he wanted to defeat the tribes in battle, and then leave them broken and powerless. We can presume that Caracalla directed the operations to continue after his father's death, and that they were successful. The Maeatae and Caledonians gave no more trouble for nearly 90 years.

18

'Carausius and his Brothers'

After the death of Severus there is hardly a mention by ancient historians of events in Britain over the next 70 years or so. Severus had taken good care to prevent anyone following Albinus' example. He divided Britain into two provinces, *Britannia Superior* and *Britannia Inferior* – Upper and Lower Britain. Where the border was we do not know; but clearly its purpose was to divide the armies, and to give each half a separate commander.

Archaeological evidence also is less helpful than usual. By AD 225 the repair work which Severus had ordered was all complete, and after this date there are comparatively few inscriptions; in fact the number dwindles progressively from now onwards.

There was also, and this is not surprising, a decline in building. In the first place the town houses had nearly all been rebuilt in stone by the end of the second century, and there is no reason why these and the public buildings should not have survived at least 100 years without having to be rebuilt.

Secondly, the ramparts of earth surrounding the towns imposed a definite limit on expansion; it is unlikely that there would have been much building outside the defences, and we shall see that these defences became increasingly necessary.

But there is another reason for the lack of expansion in Britain: it is to be found in the terrible conditions which befell the rest of the empire. Barbarian invasions across its frontiers brought widespread destruction, and the cost of repelling them and repairing the damage was very great. Harsh taxation caused such unrest that in Gaul, for instance, bands of hard-pressed peasants roamed the country, burning and robbing, or hid in the woods to avoid capture; there they were joined by deserters from the armies.

Plague swept into the empire from the East, and raged for years at a time. Famine desolated huge areas of the provinces. The population fell alarmingly, and to make up for the shortage of men, barbarian mercenaries were hired to man the frontier defences. To pay for them the emperors resorted to 'inflation' of a dangerous kind. Copper coins were coated with a thin wash of silver, and issued as real silver coins. Unable to trust the coinage, men resorted to a primitive system of barter.

The chaos was not confined to economic affairs. The emperors became

The town wall of Silchester

weaker and weaker, the armies more and more independent of central control. Between AD 235 and AD 284 over 50 Augusti and Caesars were created – nearly all nominees of one army or another – and only one is reputed to have died a natural death.

In AD 259 a separate Empire of the Gauls was proclaimed, and lasted for 15 years; twice again, for short periods, Gaul and Spain broke away from the main empire. On all occasions Britain was governed from Gaul, without being seriously involved. Here the real danger came from raids on the south and east coasts made by fleets of Saxon and Frankish pirates.

The measures taken to deal with this menace indicate how seriously it was regarded. From about AD 250 onwards the earth ramparts round the towns were replaced by massive walls of stone. This could not have been done without specific permission from some emperor; nor would any-one have allowed such an expensive undertaking unless it had seemed really necessary. More proof comes from the number of hoards of coins buried for safety's sake *and never reclaimed.* These can of course be dated fairly precisely, and the number rises dramatically around AD 270.

At last a strong emperor emerged, who set about restoring peace and security with vigour and determination. He was Diocletian, a humbly-born soldier, who had served in the imperial bodyguard. Chosen by his fellows to avenge the murder of the emperor, he fought for the throne himself, and won. He chose as his Caesar a man called Maximian, and gave him the task of recovering Gaul and Germany. In turn Maximian chose as his commander

The main gate of Verulamium probably looked like this

of the Channel fleet – the *Classis Britannica* – a Belgian named Carausius. The historian Eutropius briefly records his story:

'At this time Carausius, a man of humble birth, won an impressive reputation for his energetic and skilful service. He was based at Boulogne, and his task was to secure the whole north coast of Gaul and Germany, which was being raided by Franks and Saxons. He often captured large numbers of these barbarians, but the booty which he took from them untouched was neither returned to the provincials, nor reached the emperor. The suspicion arose that he purposely let the raiders in to attack so that he could intercept them with their booty on the way back, and so line his own pockets. When Maximian ordered his execution, he proclaimed himself emperor, and occupied Britain.'

This occurred in AD 287: how Carausius was able to do this, and why the legions supported his claims we just do not know. He even kept control of the north coast of Gaul, and Maximian was defeated and driven off when he tried to regain control. Diocletian and Maximian were then so occupied with other, more serious wars against the invading Franks and Saracens that they could do nothing but accept the situation. Eutropius has the reasons right, but some of the details wrong, in his account:

'So, since the whole world was in a turmoil, with Carausius rebelling in Britain and Achilleus in Egypt, when the Pentepolitani (in Cyrenaica) were raiding

Africa (the Roman province along the north coast of the continent), and
Narseus, (king of Persia) was invading the east, Diocletian promoted Maximian
from Caesar to Augustus, and Constantius and Galerius to the rank of Caesar.
But in the end he made peace with Carausius, for his campaigns against this man,
so skilled in all matters of war, had been in vain.'

Such an enormous amount of work confronted Diocletian after the chaos
of the previous 50 years that he had to divide the office of emperor. The two
Augusti, with Caesars as adjutants and intended successors, governed different parts of the empire. Each part was in turn divided into *dioceses*, in
the care of a *vicarius*, and each diocese into provinces. Britain became a
diocese divided into four provinces, *Britannia Prima*, *Britannia Secunda*, *Maxima
Caesariensis* and *Flavia Caesariensis*. Diocletian was still the master, and to
cement the new arrangement he compelled the new Caesars to divorce their
wives and marry the daughters of the Augusti!

Naturally Diocletian and Maximian did not advertise their failure, but
Carausius was quick to announce his success. He issued a splendid series of
coins, with legends like 'The Peace of the Three Emperors', and 'The
Happiness of our Times', and even one showing the heads of Diocletian,
Maximian and Carausius, with the legend 'Carausius and his Brothers.'

But the most lasting effect of Carausius' rule is still here for us to see. The
Saxon pirate fleets had grown stronger and bolder – the Channel fleet could
no longer control them. Sidonius Apollinaris, a bishop and statesman of the
fifth century, had a healthy respect for them:
'Of all our enemies they are the most savage. They attack without warning, and
sail away if warning is given. They brush aside resistance, and butcher the
unwary. No ship can outsail them in flight or pursuit. They do not fear
shipwreck, but rather regard it as a useful experience. They do not merely know
the perils of the sea – they actually welcome them.

'Stormy weather encourages landsmen to believe they are safe from attack, but
the Saxons are then safe from observation, and dash happily through waves and
treacherous rocks in the hope of an attack.

'Before they shake out their sails, weigh anchor from the enemy beaches and
make for home from the continent, it is their custom to drown or hang one in
ten of their captives. They do this for religious reasons, which makes it all the
more horrifying. They draw lots over the assembled crowd of victims – a fair
system for an unfair death.'

Richborough from the air

Against these pirates Carausius was forced to extend the defence system along the coasts of Gaul, Germany and Britain, and began the building of a series of great forts, known as 'the Forts of the Saxon Shore'. (See p. 151.)

These were of a new and advanced design. The corners are square, not rounded. The internal towers give way to huge, drumlike bastions built on to the outside of the walls. In the top of the bastions are sockets for spring-

The walls of Burgh Castle

loaded guns, with a range of up to 200 yards. In front of the walls a wide, shallow ditch delayed the enemy while he was at the mercy of the guns.

The position of the forts is no less significant. They all guard strategically important points along the coasts – harbours and river estuaries. From these, too, Roman warships could race out to grapple with the Saxons. They are a part of naval, not military, policy, as their sites prove. They are not positioned on important roads; some were obviously manned and supplied entirely by sea. Even today, when the receding seas have left them marooned in fields of green, their commanding walls and great towers cannot fail to stir the imagination. The three most worth a visit are at Porchester, Pevensey and Richborough, all in the care of the Ministry of Public Building and Works.

The fort at Porchester

The Roman Pharos, or lighthouse, still overlooks the harbour at Dover

Eventually Constantius found time and troops to move north, and in AD 293 he took Carausius' base at Boulogne. Before Carausius could recover, he was murdered by Allectus, his chief finance officer. Allectus ruled in Britain for three years, and for a time was recognised by the Augusti. One of his coins bears the legend 'Allectus and his Brothers', and 'The Peace of the Three Augusti.'

His defeat at the hands of Constantius in AD 296 is told in one of a series of 12 'Panegyrics' – compositions full of flattery and mythological comparisons supposedly addressed to several emperors in honour of some memorable event. The seventh was written for Constantius' defeat of Allectus. It is a strange, repetitive and awkward piece of writing. But it did inspire a fine paragraph in Gibbon's *Decline and Fall of the Roman Empire*.

'The attack was at length made by the principal squadron, which under the command of the prefect Asclepiodotus, an officer of distinguished merit, had been assembled at the mouth of the Seine. So imperfect in those times was the art of navigation that orators have celebrated the daring courage of the Romans, who ventured to set sail with a side wind, and on a stormy day. The weather proved favourable to their enterprise. Under the cover of a thick fog, they escaped the fleet of Allectus, which had been stationed off the Isle of Wight to receive them, landed in safety on some part of the Western coast, and convinced the Britons that a superiority of naval strength will not always protect their country from a foreign invasion. Asclepiodotus had no sooner disembarked the imperial troops than he set fire to his ships; and, as the expedition proved fortunate, his heroic

149

The medallion of
Constantius Chlorus

conduct was universally admired. The usurper had posted himself near London, to expect the formidable attack of Constantius, who commanded in person the fleet of Boulogne; but the descent of a new enemy required his immediate presence in the West. He performed this long march in so precipitate a manner that he encountered the whole force of the prefect with a small body of harassed and disheartened troops. The engagement was soon terminated by the total defeat and death of Allectus; a single battle, as it has often happened, decided the fate of this great island; and, when Constantius landed on the shores of Kent, he found them covered with obedient subjects. Their acclamations were loud and unanimous; and the virtues of the conqueror may induce us to believe that they were sincerely rejoiced in a revolution which, after a separation of ten years, restored Britain to the body of the Roman Empire.'

One of the gold medallions struck to commemorate this victory was found in 1922 at Arras in France. It shows Constantius on horseback being welcomed at the gates of London: the legend reads REDDITOR LUCIS AETERNAE – Restorer of Eternal Light.

Constantius indeed had much to restore. When Allectus had withdrawn troops from the frontier to meet Constantius' attack, the Picts, as the Caledonians were now known, again swept south across the wall, spreading fear and destruction. The panegyric says for AD 297 that the tribes of the far north now obeyed the emperor, but there is no other literary reference to Constantius' campaigns to push the Picts back into Scotland.

However, the damage done to the wall, and to some of the forts, milecastles and turrets, and the repair work, can still be traced. In 1929 an inscription was found at Birdoswald on the wall. It reads:

'For our Lords Diocletian and Maximian, Invincible Augusti, and for Constantius and Maximian, the noble Caesars, under His Excellence Aurelius Arpagius, the Governor, the Commanding Officer's quarters which had been covered by earth and fallen in ruins, the Headquarters building, and the bath-house, were restored by the First Aelian Cohort of Dacians under the supervision of Flavius Martinus, centurion in command.'

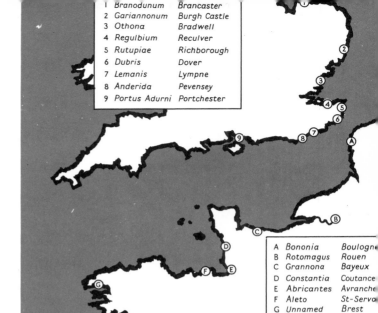

1	Branodunum	Brancaster
2	Gariannonum	Burgh Castle
3	Othona	Bradwell
4	Regulbium	Reculver
5	Rutupiae	Richborough
6	Dubris	Dover
7	Lemanis	Lympne
8	Anderida	Pevensey
9	Portus Adurni	Portchester

A	Bononia	Boulogne
B	Rotomagus	Rouen
C	Grannona	Bayeux
D	Constantia	Coutance
E	Abricantes	Avranche
F	Aleto	St-Serva
G	Unnamed	Brest

The forts of the Saxon Shore

This must have been set up before May 1st, AD 305, for on that day Diocletian and Maximian retired from office, and Constantius and Maximian became Augusti.

In AD 306 Constantius came to Britain again, now as senior Augustus, and was joined by his son Constantine. According to the panegyrist a campaign into Scotland brought a quick victory. By July Constantius was back in York, and there, like Severus before him, attended by his son, he died on July 25th.

There is an unspoken summary of the whole story on a milestone found near Carlisle. On one end of the six foot high column of stone are the words:

'In honour of the Imperial Caesar, Marcus Aurelius Mausaeus Carausius, Good, Fortunate and Unconquered.'

When he *was* conquered, the stone was too good to waste; it was turned upside down, and on the other end, opposite way up, we can read:

'In honour of Flavius Valerius Constantine, the noble Caesar.'

When this Constantine came to the throne, he did more than any other emperor to encourage the growth of Christianity. It is time now to look more closely at the ordinary people of the Roman world, and at the gods they believed in.

19

Men and Gods

The religion of Rome was simple, and did not demand very much from its citizens. There were a number of gods, like Jupiter and Venus, Mars and Diana; the official state religion was the worship of these gods. Temples were built in their honour, to house a statue of the god, before which offerings could be made. It was hoped that in return for these gifts the gods would protect the state and make it prosper.

There were also some other gods, more personal and private, whose help could be sought and whose evils must be averted. Best known perhaps are the Penates, Vesta and Lares, the gods of the store-cupboard, hearth and household in general.

But the state did not insist that the Roman gods and goddesses were unique. The citizens, provided that they were prepared to pay homage to the state gods, could worship as many others as they wanted, no matter how strange they were or where they came from. However, any religion which was dangerous or corrupting was banned. For example, part of the service to their gods required by the Druid priests was human sacrifice; for this reason, and for its resistance to Roman rule, it was ruthlessly stamped out, as we have seen.

Christianity, too, was at first unacceptable to Rome. The Christians, like the Jews, believed that there was only one God, and refused to worship any others; their refusal to accept the divinity of the emperors was particularly galling. Temples to the reigning emperor were often built in the provinces, like that of Claudius at Colchester. The worship of the emperor, coupled with that of the spirit of Rome, was encouraged as one means of unifying the diverse peoples of the Roman world.

Again, a religion which taught, 'Blessed are the meek: for they shall inherit the earth', and, 'But many that are first shall be last; and the last shall be first', was not likely to be popular with the rulers of a society which relied on slaves to do its hard work. Such beliefs partly explain why the less fortunate inhabitants of the empire were among the first to embrace Christianity.

Almost all the evidence for the pagan religions of Roman Britain comes from the inscriptions on altars and offerings to the various gods. The Celtic gods were not only worshipped by the native Britons, but also by the soldiers and civilians who came here from all quarters of the empire. Such gods are

Maponus, Cocidius, Anociticus and Vitiris. Their worship only extended over small areas of the country, and sometimes for only a few years.

Most famous of them all, perhaps, was Nodens, a god of hunting and healing. A great shrine was built to him at Lydney, in Gloucestershire, at the end of the fourth century, during the temporary revival of paganism under the emperor Julian. Behind a large temple, not unlike a Christian church, was a long, narrow building with a number of small rooms, believed to be for visiting worshippers. Nearby was a large guest house built round a court-yard, and a bath-house of typically Roman type.

Thousands of brooches, pins and bracelets, offered by high and low, rich and poor, to Nodens show how popular he was. On one of them, a small piece of pewter, two by three inches, in clumsy, inaccurate Latin, is written:

'To the god Nodens. Silvianus has lost his ring. He has dedicated half its value to Nodens. Please allow no health among those with the name Senicianus until he brings it back to Nodens' temple.'

Senicianus is a very unusual name. A gold ring found at Silchester bears the inscription 'Senicianus, Live in God', and this is a Christian relic. It is very hard not to believe that this is the very ring in question, though this would be an extraordinary coincidence.

These Celtic gods are often identified with Roman ones; near Carlisle an altar was dedicated to Mars Cocidius by men of the Second Augustan Legion. A centurion of the same legion put up four dedication stones which show that little distinction was made between native and Roman gods. One is to Jupiter Optimus Maximus, one to Apollo and Diana, another to 'Mars and Minerva, the Guardians of the parade ground, Epona (a Gallic horse-god) and Victory', and a fourth to 'The Spirit of the Land of Britain'. The centurion was certainly taking no chances!

Even well-born and influential Romans did not despise the local gods. A dedication was found at Benwell, on Hadrian's wall:

'To the god Anociticus (this stone was set up) by Tineius Longus who, while serving as Prefect of Cavalry under the consular governor Ulpius Marcellus, by the decision of our Best and Greatest Emperors, was decorated with the Broad Stripe, and promoted Quaestor.'

153

A Romano-Celtic temple

The 'broad stripe' is the broad purple stripe of the white toga; it is the distinguishing mark of the senatorial class to which the grateful Tineius has just been promoted.

Not only Roman and Celtic gods were honoured. A late inscription from York testifies to the arrival not only of eastern gods, but also of the foreigners who worshipped them:

'To the holy god Serapis this temple was built from the ground by Claudius Hieronymianus, Legate of the Sixth Legion, Victorious.'

Hieronymus is a Greek name, here romanised by the ending – *ianus*.

In this country perhaps the most important foreign god is Mithras; five temples have been found, three on the Wall, one at Caernavon, and one famous site in London. You can still see the foundations of it in Queen Victoria Street, near the Mansion House in London, preserved in a modern setting. The temples were small and narrow; at one end was the sanctuary

Mithras
slaying
the bull

Silver vessels found
in the temple of
Mithras in London

of the god, often with a relief recording the feat of Mithras when he slew a wild bull, whose death brought light to the earth. Some of the sacred silver vessels, and the relief from the London Mithraeum, can be seen in the Guildhall Museum on the High Walk over London Wall in the City of London.

The underground temples of Mithras were unusual in Britain. Most Celtic temples were tall, square buildings, surrounded on all four sides by a verandah. They were not intended to contain a congregation, but are merely the house of the god. A notable example was in the centre of Maiden Castle; beside it are the foundations of the priest's house.

There were few examples in this country of the classical temple, with its rows of columns, common in the rest of the empire. Claudius' temple at Colchester was one; another was at the health resort of Bath. A great temple was built to Sul, goddess of the hot springs; from the pediment of the temple comes the great Gorgon's head, with its Celtic face and snake-infested hair. The Latin name of Bath was *Aquae Sulis* – The Waters of Sul.

We do not know exactly when Christianity came to Britain, but Tertullian, who lived in Carthage, wrote in AD 206 that 'some places in Britain, where the Romans cannot go, have however yielded to Christ', which seems to indicate that Christianity had already spread up to, and beyond, the frontier.

But Christians were not always granted freedom of worship. The Venerable Bede, a Saxon monk who wrote a *History of the English Church* in a monastery at Jarrow during the eighth century, reports the death of Allectus, and continues:

'Meanwhile Diocletian in the East, and Maximian in the West, gave orders for the destruction of the churches, and the torture and execution of Christians; this was the tenth persecution since the time of Nero. It lasted longer and was more savage than all the others.

'At the time when the Christians were being most cruelly suppressed, in accordance with the orders of the infidel emperors, Alban received into his house one of the clergy who was in flight from his persecutors. When Alban saw him devoting himself day and night to continual prayer and watchfulness, he was suddenly touched by the grace of God, and began to follow his example of faith and piety. Little by little he learnt from his wise exhortations, and leaving behind the darkness of idolatry, he became a Christian with all his heart.'

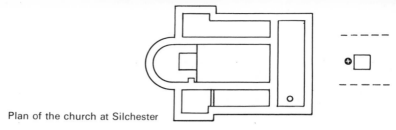

Plan of the church at Silchester

Alban was arrested and charged with harbouring the priest. He declared that he was a Christian, and refused to worship the gods of Rome. At this he was lead to a hill outside the town and beheaded. The town was Verulamium, and its name now, of course, is Saint Albans.

There were other martyrs, too, Aaron and Julius in the 'City of the Legions' – probably Caerleon. However, Diocletian rescinded the persecution before the end of his reign, and Gildas, a Welsh priest living in the sixth century, says that when it was over many of the churches were restored, and new ones built.

By now the Church in Britain was well organised, and was important enough to be asked to take part in the general affairs of the Church as a whole. In AD 314 three bishops from Britain attended the Council of Arles – the word *bishop* does not have its modern sense; it merely represents the leader of any local, but organised, group of Christians. We hear of British bishops at another Council in AD 359, in the *Sacred History* of Sulpicius Severus, a rich provincial who later became a monk:

'So officials were sent through Illyricum, Italy, Africa and the Spanish and Gallic provinces, and by invitation or compulsion over 400 bishops in the West came to a Council at Ariminum (a town in Italy). The emperor had given instructions that they were to be given a grant towards their expenses. But the bishops from my own country, Aquitaine, and from the Gallic and British provinces thought that this was not proper. They preferred to refuse the contribution from the public treasury, and to live at their own expense. Only three bishops from Britain, through lack of money of their own, made use of the official grant; they had turned down a collection offered by their congregations, for they believed it more pious to be a burden on the public treasury than on individuals.

'I have heard that the Bishop Gavidius from my own country used to refer disparagingly to this. But I would in no way agree with him, and think that it was to their credit that they were so poor that they had nothing of their own, and that they took money not from other people, but from the treasury, which did not hurt anyone. For both reasons it was a splendid example.'

Though not all her bishops had accepted the grant, the British Church at this time was obviously very poor. It is perhaps for this reason that the archaeological remains of Christianity are so small and few, while they are

A reconstruction
of the Silchester
church

so splendid on the continent. The most significant from this period is the building at Silchester identified as a church, and that is only 42 feet long and 24 feet wide. Its plan is easily recognised.

Most of the other objects that are Christian – small tombstones, for example, metal vessels, brooches and spoons – there are hardly a hundred in all, bear distinctive Christian marks. The most common is the Chi-Rho monogram. The first two letters of Christ, written in Greek, are Chi (X) and Rho (P): these are superimposed to form the sign ☧.

Famous examples come from Lullingstone, where the owner transformed one of his rooms into a chapel, and had the plaster painted with Chi–Rhos and figures standing in prayer, and from a villa in Dorset. Here, at Hinton St. Mary, there was a mosaic floor: in the centre is the head of Christ, and behind it the Chi–Rho. This was moved to the British Museum, and put on display in a magnificent position in 1967.

The Head of Christ from the villa at Hinton St. Mary

```
R O T A S
O P E R A
T E N E T
A R E P O
S A T O R
```

One of the strangest Christian relics is a word square scratched on the plaster of a house at Cirencester:

This reads the same in all four directions, and might be translated 'Arepo the sower holds the wheels carefully'; but when re-arranged, the letters read:

```
A              P              O
               A
               T
               E
               R
P A T E R   N O S T E R
               O
               S
               T
               E
O              R              A
```

Pater Noster, Our Father, are the first two words of the Lord's Prayer in Latin. The extra A and O are Alpha and Omega, the first and last letters of the Greek alphabet: 'I am Alpha and Omega, the beginning and the ending, saith the Lord.' (Revelation of St. John, i. 7.)

From the beginning of the fifth century Christianity grew rapidly in this country, as we learn from Gildas and Bede. St. Ninian's monastery at Whithorn in Wigtownshire was built in AD 397. St. Patrick was a missionary in Ireland for 30 years in the middle of the fifth century, and his father and grandfather were both Christians. In AD 429 St. Germanus came to Britain from Gaul with another bishop, and baptized many of the people.

The victory of Christianity is not surprising. In the trouble and anxieties of a Britain deprived of the strength and protection of Roman leadership and discipline, when men were left to their own faltering resources, the comfort and hope of the Christian faith, and its ideals, must have been irresistible.

20

People and Things

The population of Roman Britain was small; under 2,000,000 people lived in Roman Britain. Ancient writers have much to say about their wars and conquests; but of their private lives, whether they were Roman commanders or humble peasants, or of what they were like, they tell us almost nothing. Tacitus' description of the country and its people adds little to that of Caesar (page 14), except for this brief account of the Britons his father-in-law met:

'Of the original inhabitants of Britain, whether immigrant or aboriginal, the barbarians know very little, as one might expect. But some theories can be suggested by variations in physical appearance. The red hair and large limbs of the inhabitants of Scotland declare a German origin; the Silures have swarthy features, and very often curly hair: this, and the position of their country opposite Spain, makes it credible that their ancestors crossed from there and occupied their present position. Those nearest to the Gauls are also like them; this is either because the original strain has persisted, or because geographical position determines physical characteristics, since the two countries stretch towards each other.'

The writers may tell us little, but from archaeology we can learn a great deal. Finds of Roman-type pottery, tools, toilet articles and inscriptions from all over the country show that the inhabitants soon adopted Roman imports and habits, and even the Latin language. While the Celts used their native tongue in conversation, they wrote in Latin. An indignant tile-maker in London, for instance, scratched in the still wet clay, with two or three spelling mistakes:

'Austalis has been wandering off on his own every day for a fortnight.'

A tombstone from Wroxeter has three panels, with Latin inscriptions. On the first is:

'To the memory of Placida, aged 55. This stone was set up by her husband in the thirtieth year of their marriage.'

A toy chariot

On the second panel (the third was never used) is written:

'To the memory of Deuccus, aged 15. His brother put this up.'

The fact that the woman and the boy have only one name, even if, like Placida, it is of a Roman type, shows that they were Britons. But everything about the stone itself demonstrates how completely they have adopted Roman customs. The phrase, for example, translated here as 'To the memory of . . .' is in Latin *Dis Manibus* – to the gods of the Underworld – the conventional first line on most Roman tombstones.

The many tombstones which have survived, with their short life-histories, and the few *graffiti* – informal scratchings on walls and pieces of pottery – give us many insights into the lives of the people. We can also make sensible guesses from our knowledge of the Romans in other parts of the empire, and even from our own experience, for people have been much the same in all places and times.

Men and women meet and fall in love: at Leicester is a piece of pottery, and on it, most carefully scratched:

'Verecunda the actress, Lucius the gladiator.'

and it is not difficult to imagine two members of a touring troupe of entertainers making some permanent record of their affection.

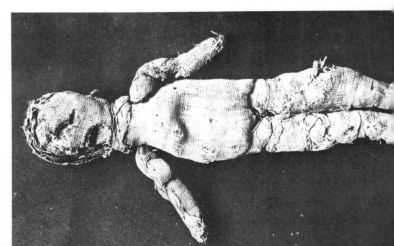

A 'rag' doll

160

Writing implements

Children were born, and left a few memories of their childhood, a toy chariot, a doll, and a doll's tea-set. Then came lessons; and the pens, inkwells and writing tablets they used have survived. But children died, too, and we should remember that in societies more primitive than ours the death rate was very high indeed; only about half of all children lived until their twentieth birthday. Here are two epitaphs:

'To the memory of Simplicia Florentina, a most innocent soul. She lived ten months. Her father Felicius Simplex, soldier of the Sixth Legion, Victorious, set this up.'

'Julia Materna, aged six. Julius Marcellinus set this up for his beloved daughter.'

Both these little girls were daughters of soldiers living in barracks, and up to one man in ten was a soldier of one sort or another; we have many of their tombstones. Here is an unusual one from the Antonine wall:

'To the memory of Nectovelius, son of Vindex, aged 30, in the ninth year of his service. He was a Brigantian tribesman, serving in the Second Thracian Cohort.'

Not many Britons served, in Britain, as soldiers of the Roman army. But not all soldiers died on active service:

'(Here lies) Julius Valens, Veteran of the Second Augustan Legion. He lived 100 years. His wife Julia Secundina and son Julius Martinus had this made.'

F

Roman balance

There was time too for more than fighting or training, as this tablet set up miles from anywhere in Durham records:

'Sacred to the Invincible Silvanus (god of the countryside). Gaius Tetius Veturius Micianus, Commander of the Sebosian cavalry wing, set this up gladly, in discharge of his vow, for the capture of a magnificent boar, which many before him were unable to catch.'

But most men in the country were farmers; their ploughshares and granaries, bill-hooks and spades, and the houses they lived in, have been found in many parts of the country. The excavations around Chilgrove, in Sussex, in 1967, where there may have been five villa farms, have indicated that farming in Roman times may have been almost as intensive as it is today.

In the towns men practised all sorts of trades and professions. A writing tablet found at Walbrook in London has *Londinio* inscribed on the outside, and on the inside, impressed right through the original wax coating into the wood, is:

'Rufus, son of Callusinus, sends greetings to Epillicus and all his associates. I think you know that I am well. If you have made the list, please send it. Look after everything carefully. Make sure to turn that slave-girl into hard cash . . .'

There were shopkeepers of all kinds, of course, and many of their balances and steel-yards, used for weighing out goods, have been found. At Verulam you can see a butcher's cleaver, and a carpenter's plane. At Silchester enough tools were found to allow a reconstruction of a carpenter's shop to be made.

An innkeeper in London was perhaps disturbed at losing too many of his wine jars, and had his address scratched on them to claim ownership. One was found with the words:

'London: next door to the Temple of Isis.' ▶

A 3rd century carpenter's shop at Silchester

The plane in use in the reconstruction above
The wooden body has perished

London innkeeper's wine-jar

163

A reconstruction of a Roman-British kitchen using models of objects found at Silchester

An oculist's stamp was found at Sandy, in Bedfordshire. On the four sides of a little flat slab are four labels; the letters are reversed – the stone was pressed into the solid cakes of ointment, leaving both the name of the ointment, and its maker:

G. VALERIUS AMANDUS	Vinegar-lotion for runny eyes.
G. VALERIUS AMANDUS	Drops for dim sight.
G. VALERIUS VALENTINUS	Poppy-salve; use after an attack of eye inflammation.
G. VALERIUS VALENTINUS	Mixture for clear eyes.

The women and housewives had much to occupy them. They saw to the spinning and weaving of clothes; loom-weights and spindles can often be seen. In Verulamium museum there are fragments of a woollen cloak, in which the body of a young boy was wrapped before he was put into his coffin. Leather was used for clothing as well. A leather bikini was brought up from a Roman well in London, and leather shoes and sandals have been recovered.

A glass bowl, not 'Pyrex'

Imported Samian ware

A colander

   Kitchen pots of every kind have been found, from saucepans to colanders. The housewife also chose the best 'china'. At first Samian ware was used. This is the name given to excellent mass-produced pottery, imported from Gaul in the first two centuries. It has a dark-red, glossy, very hard glaze. The clay was pressed round, or into, moulds, into which elaborate patterns had been cut, and these patterns were reproduced on the finished pots. The potter's name is often stamped inside, on the bottom. The changes in pattern, and the development of the styles, can be recognised, and Samian ware is very useful evidence for dating the strata in which it is found.

Sandals found in London

165

Later, British pottery replaced Samian ware; the best quality is perhaps 'Castor ware', made of grey clay, with a raised pattern of clay slip put on after the pot was formed. Pieces of rough, coarse pottery, broken in everyday use, are very common.

Some decorative glassware

But in the richest houses silver plate was used. In Suffolk, in 1939, a plough turned up a superb dinner service of imported silver plate, hidden in the ground to preserve it from Saxon raiders. This Mildenhall Treasure is one of the most magnificent exhibits in the British Museum.

A comb

Cosmetic phials

The housewife, though, did not spend all her time working. The richer houses owned slaves, and the lady of the house had time to dress her hair in elaborate fashions. A host of hairpins, combs, tweezers, pins, brooches and ear-rings testify to a keen interest in her personal appearance, and little glass phials for cosmetic creams and lotions stood on dressing-tables as they do today.

A necklace

Tweezers

There is one couple who deserve especial attention. From Tyneside comes a simple tombstone:

'To the memory of Barathes of Palmyra, Veteran, who lived 68 years.'

Surely not many men came to Britain from Palmyra, a city in an oasis in a Syrian desert. But there is more of interest in Barathes than an old soldier who retired and died far from home in the chilly air of Northumberland. Nearby, at South Shields, a superb tombstone was found. The Latin inscription means:

'To the memory of Regina, of the Catuvellaunian tribe, who died aged 30, freedwoman and wife of Barates of Palmyra (who set this up).'

Underneath, in Palmyrene script, is written:

'Regina, freedwoman of Barates. Alas!'

Regina sits in a wicker chair, wearing bracelets and a necklace: she holds a distaff and spindle, and an open jewel box. By her right foot is a casket with a large keyhole, and by her left her work-basket, with her balls of wool.

It would seem that after his discharge from the army Barates became a trader, and a successful one too, for his wife's tombstone must have been very expensive. At some time in his career he bought a British slave-girl in East Anglia, and took her to his home in the North. He became fond of her, gave her freedom, and made her his lawful wife. Something of his lonely sorrow can be felt in that one, sad line of Palmyrene. How many people, apart from Barates himself, can have understood it?

A soldier from a Syrian oasis, and a slave-girl of Belgic descent, who had lived in East Anglia, buried in the north of England near a wall designed by an Emperor of Rome who had been born in Spain – Roman Britain may seem a strange mixture to us, but the unity of different elements, with no barriers of race or creed, was typical of the Roman Empire, and to a large extent responsible for its strength.

The tombstone of Regina

Menace from Abroad

When Constantius died at York in AD 306 he left Britain in the care of his son Constantine, who was to become one of Rome's greatest emperors. Believing that Diocletian's division of the empire into four parts was wrong, he defeated his rivals one by one, to become sole emperor in AD 323. In the battles he wore the Chi–Rho as the badge on his helmet, and his troops carried it proudly on their shields. He guaranteed freedom of worship for the Christians, but was not baptized himself till shortly before his death in AD 337. He transferred the capital of the empire from Rome to Constantinople, where for four years his builders had been labouring in the making of a splendid new city. Constantinople means 'Constantine's City'.

But his first claim to the throne from York had not gone unchallenged; he was forced to return to the continent and fight for the title. Britain was left to a period of great prosperity, probably unequalled in the rest of the Roman world. The reasons are many.

In the general anarchy of the third century, prices had risen again and again. A measure of corn, worth 8 drachmae in the old days, had in Egypt risen to 120,000 drachmae! Diocletian's remedy was one we would recognize today; he issued a list of the maximum prices for a whole range of goods. Some trades and professions then became unprofitable, and the men practising them tried to change their jobs. Restrictions were introduced, and a control of labour was enforced; in the end, sons were forbidden to do anything but follow their fathers' trades. These stern measures did work, for stability and some prosperity returned to most parts of the empire.

Britain was lucky, and was spared the devastations of the barbaric invasions. Moreover, in the past, much of the country's income had gone overseas in purchasing imports. But the industries established in Britain had flourished, and by this time home products were fortunately replacing imports.

The Spanish tin mines had been worked out, and the increasing number of milestones of the fourth century found in Cornwall is evidence of the renewed interest of Rome in British tin. Lead had always been easily produced in this country; now it was mixed with tin to form pewter, and tableware of this metal became common, only replaced by silver plate in the very richest houses.

An aerial view of remains of the villa at Chedworth

As agricultural methods improved, regular surpluses of grain could be exported. We are told that in AD 359 the emperor Julian had 800 barges built to carry corn from Britain to relieve Gallic cities after the barbarian devastations. British woollen goods, too, were popular, and two of them, a duffle coat and a travelling-rug, were specifically mentioned in Diocletian's fixed-price list.

Less wine was imported; not only were grapes grown in British vineyards, but one might guess that beer was beginning to replace it in popular demand. The drinking vessels of the period often contain over a quart – hardly suitable for wine! – and Diocletian's price list mentions British beer at 4 denarii a pint.

But the most obvious example of prosperity can be found in the town and country houses of this century. For the first time really magnificent villas of great size, with extensive hypocaust systems and fine mosaics, were built in the countryside, most of them in the west country. Up to 70 have been discovered, and they were very rich estates indeed. The modern house built in the villa at Chedworth is dwarfed by the earlier estate. Bath-houses were built, not only for the villa owner, but for the staff as well, as at the villa at Bignor in Sussex; there must have been a large number of estate workers, for it has been estimated that 2,000 acres were under cultivation. The original villa of the second century is only a tiny part of the later complex of rooms.

A model of the villa at Lullingstone

Mosaic from Lullingstone: Bellerephon slaying the Chimaera

The wall of the Pevensey fort: the castle is mediaeval

At Verulamium the theatre was reconstructed and enlarged, after a period when it seems to have been neglected. The Basilica of Silchester was completely rebuilt, and the baths extensively modified in the middle of the century, as were those of Canterbury some years later. These are important indications; men will spend money on their own homes, but only when they have some to spare will they devote it to the needs of the community as a whole.

No hint of trouble is heard of until AD 342, when the emperor Constans, son of Constantine, made a quick dash to the island in mid-winter, though we do not know the reason. But the fort of Pevensey was added to the forts of the Saxon shore at this time; a coin which could not have been minted before AD 334 was found *under* one of the bastions.

By AD 360 the threat was greater. Our source is Ammianus Marcellinus, an historian possibly as remarkable as Tacitus, who wrote at the very end of the fourth century.

'In Britain the savage tribes of the Scots and Picts broke the treaties they had made: their raids and the devastation of the lands in the frontier region terrified the provincials, who were already exhausted by the series of previous disasters. The Caesar, Julian, who was spending the winter in Paris . . . decided to send Lupercinus, his commander-in-chief at the time, to settle the troubles, either by diplomatic or military means.'

Five years later further disasters were inflicted on the British by the Picts, Saxons, Scots and Attacotti, acting independently. But this was small stuff. In AD 367 for the first time the various barbarians united, and co-ordinated their plans; their synchronised attacks were devastating:

'While hurrying towards Trier, the emperor Valentinian was alarmed by serious news that the provinces of Britain had been brought to a desperate plight by a conspiracy of the barbarians: Nectaridus, Count of the Saxon Shore, had been killed, and the general, Fullofaudes, had been caught in an ambush.'

Two men were sent to deal with the situation, but failed:

'Finally, because of the alarming events which were constantly reported from that same island, Theodosius, a man with an outstandingly successful military reputation, was selected and sent there without a moment's delay. He enrolled some legions and cohorts of brave young men, and hurried off. His success was confidently expected, even before he arrived.

'At this time the Picts, who were divided into two tribes, the Dicalydonians and the Venturions, together with the Attacotti, a nation of warriors, and the Scots, were wandering all over the country, inflicting great devastation. The shores of Gaul, wherever a raid by land or sea was possible, were being harried by the Franks and their neighbours the Saxons; they robbed and burnt without mercy, and murdered all their captives.

'To put an end to all this, if only a favourable providence should give him the chance, this most competent general headed for the world's end and came to the coast of Boulogne: this is separated from the land opposite by a narrow, tidal sea, which is accustomed to rise up in frightful surges, and then sink back into a dead calm, when sailing is absolutely safe.

'From Boulogne he calmly crossed to Richborough, a quiet post opposite. When the four units of the field army which were with him had landed, all confident in their strength, he set out and marched to London, the old town later called Augusta. Dividing his divisions into many detachments, he attacked the wandering bands of the enemy bent on destruction and weighed down with their baggage. He quickly overcame those who were driving along bound captives and cattle, and stripped them of the booty they had taken from the unfortunate provincials; he restored it all to them, except for a small part which he gave to his weary soldiers.

174

'Then joyfully, as if celebrating an ovation, he entered the city, which, though it had been submerged by the deepest calamities, recovered more quickly than relief could have been expected.

'Encouraged by his success to more adventurous exploits, he paused, while devising safe plans, in some anxiety for the future, for he had found out from the confessions of his captives and information from deserters, that the scattered masses of the enemy, made up of various tribes and frightfully savage, could only be beaten by cunning, secrecy and sudden raids. In the end, by issuing proclamations and promising free pardons, he recalled the deserters to the standards, as well as many others scattered throughout the country on indefinite leave. At this summons most were induced to come back.'

Clearly there was utter confusion in the province, from north to south. Many soldiers had openly deserted; others had not returned from leave, either confident that their claims that it was *indefinite* leave could not be disproved – a situation which argues the loss of many records and the death of many officers – or simply panic-stricken. And among these deserters there were bound to have been many runaway slaves and tenant farmers, tied by Diocletian's labour controls to the land like feudal serfs.

The whole province had been overrun; the wall was severely damaged yet again, and all its associated forts with their civilian settlements were destroyed. But in the south it seems likely that the towns had been protected by their walls, and that it was the villas in the countryside which suffered most. In any case Theodosius was thorough in his reconstruction.

'But Theodosius, that famous general, full of energy and enthusiasm, set out from Augusta, formerly called London, with an army skilfully and vigorously assembled. To the downcast and troubled fortunes of the British he brought great help: he marched ahead of the barbarians and occupied suitable spots to ambush them, never ordering the rank and file to a task without cheerfully setting an example himself. In this way he both performed the duties of an active common soldier, and shouldered the cares of a famous general.

'He routed and put to flight the various tribes who were insolent enough to attack the Romans, thinking their boldness would go unpunished. He completely restored the cities and the forts which had been founded to secure a long peace, but had again and again suffered serious damage.'

The tower added to the walls of York by Theodosius

To make Theodosius' task even more difficult, he had to contend with a conspiracy of a certain Valentinus who had been exiled to Britain for serious crimes. He had bribed the soldiers and planned rebellion. Theodosius had him executed, but did not pursue enquiries any further, to avoid stirring up more trouble.

'When this danger was completely removed – and everyone admitted that his luck had never failed him – he turned his attention again to reconstruction. He restored the cities and forts, as I mentioned before, defending the frontiers with watch-towers and guard-posts. He recovered that province which had fallen under the enemy's sway, and restored it to its former state so efficiently that he could report that it had a civil governor. It was named Valentia after this, at the emperor's wish, as if he had won a triumph over it.'

This Valentia was a fifth province in Britain, named after the emperor Valentinian, but we are not very certain where it was; probably somewhere in the north of England, it was important enough to have a consular governor.

Nearly every part of the country felt the effects of Theodosius' efforts. The outpost forts, north of the Wall, were abandoned. Ammianus tells us that the frontier patrols which had been based on them, had been bribed by the enemy not to disclose the signs of the impending attack they must have seen, and they were disbanded.

The civil settlements – and 34 are known in Northumberland alone – were never rebuilt. The forts along the Wall were clumsily repaired, and men, women and children all lived inside them; some granaries and headquarters buildings were taken over for the purpose. The frontier guards manning the Wall were now not full-time soldiers, but soldier-settlers. They held their land by their military service when called upon, and farmed it in something like a feudal system of tenure.

The coasts were guarded by watch-towers up to 100 feet high. Five have been recognised in Yorkshire, at Huntcliff, Goldsborough, Ravenscar, Scarborough and Filey, and there were probably others on the west coast as well. Camouflaged scout-ships kept track on raiders until the heavier war-ships, summoned from the watch-towers, could drive them away.

It was almost certainly at this time that the town walls were modified. Bastions for defensive artillery were added, like those of the Saxon shore forts. The country was now on the defensive; Theodosius' arrangement admits that barbarian raids could not be prevented. Everyone was to flock into the towns at the first sign of danger, and wait till the raiders departed. The towns were impregnable; the invaders, at this time at any rate, were not able to organise a siege to starve them into surrender, nor had the equip-ment to breach the massive walls.

Great though the damage had been, the recovery, as Ammianus remarked, was surprisingly quick. As far as we can tell, the end of the fourth century, in town and country alike, was as prosperous as ever before.

The signal tower at Scarborough

22

The Break with Rome

The peace that Theodosius had won did not last very long. One of his lieutenants, a Spaniard named Magnus Maximus, probably as governor of this island, did something really memorable and striking (though we do not know what), for he survives in Welsh legend as Maxen Wledig, the ancestor of several lines of Welsh kings. Then, in AD 383, his ambitions could not be concealed any longer. Paulus Orosius, a Christian historian and pupil of St. Augustine, records:

'Maximus, a man of energy and honour, who was not unworthy of the office of Augustus, if only he had not broken his sacred oath by seizing supreme power, was proclaimed emperor by the army in Britain, almost against his own wishes, and crossed to Gaul. The Emperor of the West, Gratian, alarmed by his sudden invasion, was still contemplating retreat into Italy, when he was outwitted and killed.'

The empire had again been divided, and the Emperor of the East was Theodosius, son of the Theodosius who came to Britain. Gratian was succeeded as Emperor of the West by his brother Valentinian, though still only a young boy. They were too busy elsewhere to deal with Maximus, and made an agreement with him, recognising him as Augustus of Spain, Gaul and Britain. But in AD 387 Maximus broke the agreement and invaded Italy:

'Maximus drove Gratian's brother Valentinian out of Italy; he fled to the East, and was given a fond and fatherly welcome by Theodosius; later he was restored to power.'

Maximus' defeat at the hands of Theodosius in AD 388, far away in north Italy, may seem remote from Britain. But Maximus' troops had come from this country; they were not sent back. The depleted forces in Britain were unable to cope with their old enemies. A few scant references by the poet Claudian gives us some idea of what happened. He wrote a poem in honour of Stilicho, the Vandal general, when he became consul in AD 400. The provinces are fancifully depicted as human figures, lining up to sing his praises:

'Then Britain, clothed in the skin of some Scottish bear, with tattooed cheeks, and a deep blue cloak sweeping in waves to her ankles, spoke: "When the neighbouring tribes were about to kill me, I, too, was protected by Stilicho. The Scots had aroused all Ireland against me, and the sea foamed beneath the oars of the enemy. But thanks to his care I need not fear the Scots, nor tremble at the Picts, nor watch from all my shores, no matter what the wind, for the coming of the Saxons." '

It is clear that once again Britain's barbarian enemies had taken advantage of her weakness to attack, and that a Roman force, either sent or led by Stilicho, had saved her. Unfortunately little archaeological evidence has yet been recognised which can shed much light on these events.

But soon the desperate shortage of troops in the empire brought more troubles for Britain. In AD 401 the Goths were threatening Italy; Claudian tells how Stilicho suppressed a threatened rebellion north of the Alps. The troops ran to congratulate him:

'. . . next came the legion which had been defending the north of Britain, which had subdued the fierce Scots, and gazed at the strange shapes tattooed on the faces of the dying Picts.'

Stilicho had been forced to withdraw troops from this country. The remnants were unable to carry out their duties properly, or even defend themselves. Moreover, despite their loyalty to the empire as a whole, they were reluctant to leave their homes and families when a fresh summons came. The army mutinied, and chose a certain Marcus to lead them, but soon killed him in favour of a Briton named Gratian. Bede tells the story:

'When the tribes of the Alans, Suevi and Vandals, with many others, had beaten the Franks, they crossed the Rhine; while they were rampaging over all Gaul, in the province of Britain a native called Gratian was declared emperor, and then killed. A common soldier named Constantine was chosen in his place, not because he had any special skill, but simply in the hope of his name. As soon as he came to power he crossed to Gaul.'

Constantine must have had some qualities which Bede failed to recognise. Like many of our leaders in the centuries to come he realised that there could be no safety for Britain if the lands across the Channel were held by an enemy. It says much for his leadership that he could persuade the troops to follow him to the continent. Bede continues:

'There he was a positive danger to the state, for he was no match for the tricks of the barbarians, who often broke the treaties they made. So the emperor Honorius despatched Count Constant into Gaul with an army; he blockaded Constantine in the town of Arles, took him and killed him.'

Those Britons who had tried to keep the army in the island were, in the event, proved right. The Chronicle of Prosper Tiro, another of St. Augustine's disciples, tells us that in AD 410 Britain was laid waste by a Saxon invasion. Maximus, Stilicho and now Constantine had drained the country of its man-power. Unable to defend themselves the Britons sent to Rome for help:

'And Honorius sent letters to the cities in Britain, encouraging them to look to their own defence.'

Honorius could hardly do anything else, for in AD 410 Rome itself was sacked by the Goths. But Honorius' reply, recorded for us by Zosimus, a Byzantine scholar, finally removed all hope that the province could be recovered. We know little of what happened in the following years. Gildas and Bede tell of two appeals to Rome for help, and that these were answered, (perhaps the visits of Theodosius and St. Germanus are meant). The bar-barians again attacked:

'So again the wretched survivors sent a letter to Agitius, a man of Roman power, which read, "To Agitius, three times consul, the groans of the Britons:", and went on, a little later, with the complaint, "The barbarians force us to the sea, and the sea forces us back to the barbarians; between these two types of death we are slaughtered or drowned." But no help came in reply.'

Agitius is presumably Aetius, supreme commander in the West from AD 433 to 454, who was consul for the third time in AD 446.

We are also told that in these confused times a native king arose in Britain, Vortigern, and that he gave land in East Anglia to a group of Saxons in return for their help against the barbarians. But later these Saxons turned against their hosts, and with reinforcements from their homeland overran south-east England.

A vein of truth runs through all this, but we cannot tell how strong it is. The Roman historians, for their part however, had no doubts. Procopius, a contemporary of Gildas, but writing in Constantinople, declares:

'Constantine was defeated in battle and killed. Despite this, the Romans were never able to recover Britain; after this time it was ruled by usurpers.'

At some time, then, before AD 410 Britain had ceased to be a province of the Roman Empire. This break with Rome is not to be marked by the departure of Roman troops; there were many other provinces which had not been policed by the legions, and only saw troops in ceremonial visits. It is the end of the civil administration of the province by officials of the central government in Rome that really marks the rupture between Britain and the rest of the empire. Honorius did not write to his governors or procurators, nor to any of his officials, for there were none. He wrote to the *cities* – the Britons were on their own.

But contact with Rome, of one sort at any rate, was not entirely lost. Christianity flourished as the material situation grew worse. To settle a theological argument, Germanus, Bishop of Auxerre, and Lupus, Bishop of Troyes, were sent from France by the Church in Rome. Bede recounts that while they were here the Britons had to face united forces of Picts and Scots. The Bishops were asked to help; during Lent they were baptizing the soldiers:

'And when the holy days of Easter were past, the greater part of the army, fresh from baptism, took up arms to make ready for battle. Germanus declared himself their general.'

Germanus cunningly placed his men, and waited:

'Now the fierce host of the enemy came near; its approach was seen by those sitting in ambush. Suddenly Germanus himself, their standard bearer, warns them all, and bids them reply to his voice with a single shout. The enemy were unsuspecting, sure they were unobserved. Three times the priests call out,

"Alleluia". Then follows the single voice of them all, and their shout is lifted up and re-echoes from the hills around them. The host of the enemy is stricken with terror; trembling at the rocks that surround them, and at the fabric of heaven above . . . they fly in all directions, casting their weapons away, happy to escape even without a stitch upon them; but most, headlong in flight, are swallowed by the river which lay behind them.'

We know that Germanus really did come to Britain in AD 429, but we cannot even guess at the events which gave birth to the story of the 'Alleluia victory'. At any rate, Roman leadership was still valued and respected.

The Roman way of life did not come to an end in this country at the same time as its Roman government. As we might expect, the stout town walls, remodelled only a few years before by Theodosius, continued to provide splendid protection for the people so long as they were prepared to man them. Life went on behind them, even if the luxury imports from the continent ceased.

At Verulamium, for example, fine houses were still being built at the end of the fourth century. In one house a mosaic floor was sacrificed to provide a corn-drying oven, and this is unlikely to have happened while the country-side could still provide this service. This house was then replaced by a barn. When this in turn was demolished, the site was crossed by a wooden water pipe, its joints secured by iron collars, which were found in their original position only a few years ago.

So well into the fifth century building of some sort was still going on in Verulamium, and a municipal water supply was still being operated from the aqueducts. And Verulamium, remember, was much more open to attack from sea-borne raiders than towns far inland.

Equally, we should expect the villas to perish much more quickly than the towns. In the first place they were at the mercy of raiding bands; the villa at Lullingstone, for example, *was* destroyed by fire. Secondly, their survival as working estates depended on the large numbers of slaves or tenant farmers to work them. These were desperately conscripted into the armies of Maximus and Constantine, or ran away to fend for themselves. So villas were often simply deserted, as their owners moved into the towns for the protection offered by the walls. At Bignor, for instance, the rafters rotted, and collapsed, and the roof tiles were found lying on the floors.

Magonus Sucatus Patricius, better known as St. Patrick of Ireland, died either in AD 461 or 492. Though ashamed of his rustic Latin, he was proud to think of himself as a Roman citizen. His father was a decurion, and a deacon of the Christian church, 'of the village of Bannavem Taburniae: he had a country seat nearby, and there I was taken captive'. Patrick was captured by raiders, and sold into slavery in Ireland with thousands of his compatriots. After six years he escaped to Gaul, where he studied to become a priest. When, years later, he returned to Britain, his parents were still living as before, and the organisation of their little town was unchanged.

And Gildas, in AD 540, though he knew nothing of villas, for by then they had disappeared, still spoke of towns, and even talks of Latin as 'our tongue'. But enough. When Vortigern, Hengist and Horsa, even Arthur with his cavalry, enter the scene, Roman Britain has gone, and the England of the Angles is taking its place.

Finding out

Most of the important statements about Roman Britain made by ancient authors have been quoted in this book. These statements cannot change. But every year new archaeological discoveries are made; these help us to a better understanding, and sometimes a new interpretation, of the literary evidence, and gradually fill in the very many large gaps in our knowledge. This chapter explains how to find out what these discoveries are and where they are made. All over the country, too, there are Roman remains worth visiting, both in our towns and countryside, and in local and national museums, and tracking these down can be a fascinating occupation.

The first essential is the *Ordnance Survey Map of Roman Britain*. This superb map shows the sites of all the remains that have been found, from a villa to a coin, whether they are still visible or not. The map is part of a booklet, and this explains all the symbols used to distinguish the finds, and lists the map references for all the important ones. There are separate maps in the booklet for areas of special interest; with its brief historical survey, it does everything possible to give an over-all picture of Roman civilisation in this country.

Also published by the Ordnance Survey is the two-inch-to-one-mile map of Hadrian's Wall, invaluable for anyone who wants to find out more about the greatest remnant of the Roman Empire in this country.

But a word of warning. Read as much as you can about the site you want to visit, and try to learn everything that is known about it. 'Roman ruins' can often be disappointing – a bump in the ground, or a few low stone walls; only if you understand what they are, will the ruins 'come to life', and if your imagination is not stirred, your visit will only be wasted. Many sites, too, are on private land, and although most owners are glad to allow access to the site if permission is first sought by letter, this is, of course, not always the case.

For news of archaeological discoveries, look in national and local newspapers, especially *The Times*, *The Daily Telegraph* and *The Guardian*. In the summer and autumn months, when the digs are carried out, there are often articles describing and explaining the latest finds, though you will have to scour the pages carefully to make sure not to miss them. Magazines like *The Illustrated London News* and *The Field* occasionally have reports of interest-

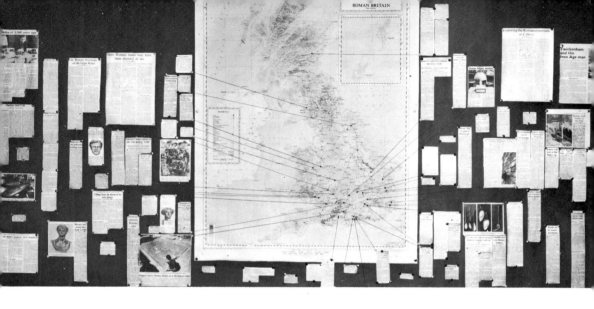

ing excavations; your local library is the place to find them. The newspaper articles collected in one term by a small class of boys are shown in the photograph; they have been linked to the relevant place on an unfolded paper version of the Ordnance Survey map by thin twine and map tacks.

A list of all the previous year's excavations, with a separate record of all newly found inscriptions, appears each year in *The Journal of Roman Studies*, published by The Society for the Promotion of Roman Studies, 31–34 Gordon Square, W.C.1. Off-prints of this section of the Journal can be obtained. Schools are often members of the Society. This journal also contains news and reviews of recent books about Roman Britain; but remember, it contains highly specialised articles for adult scholars, and much of it may be hard for laymen to understand. In 1971 the Society also began to issue an annual journal devoted entirely to Roman Britain, called *Britannia*, and this is indispensable for serious scholars.

The surest source of information about archaeological activities in your district is probably your local Museum, or, failing that, your local library. In most counties, too, there are Archaeological or History Societies; some of these have special sections for younger enthusiasts. Most of them publish their own journals (sometimes called 'Proceedings', or 'Transactions',) with news of local discoveries and excavations.

Other information can be obtained from *The Council for British Archaeology*, of 8 St. Andrew's Place, London, N.W.1. Two of its regular publications are particularly useful. First, the *Calendar of Excavations*, published every month from March to September, gives news of all forthcoming excavations.

Secondly, there is a list of *Current and Forthcoming Offprints,* published twice a year. It would be almost impossible to keep track of all the excavation reports in the journals of local archaeological societies, and very expensive to buy them all. But it is possible to select an interesting report from this list, and send a shilling or two for it. The specialist is also catered for by summaries of all the more important papers in the new series of *British Archaeological Abstracts*.

Another very attractive and valuable fund of archaeological news is to be found in *Current Archaeology,* a magazine with many excellent illustrations, which first appeared in 1967. It is published six times a year by Andrew and Wendy Selkirk, from 128, Barnsbury Road, London, N.1.

In many towns, and on the largest sites, there are museums. All of them have fascinating displays. Shortages of staff and money may sometimes be reflected in overcrowded exhibits in dreary and dusty surroundings, but it is safe to say that in all of them an intelligent interest will be warmly welcomed, and sensible questions answered with care and accuracy. Some museums, too, run a schools loan service from which a box of specimens can be borrowed for use in the classroom. But there is one service you cannot expect from a museum. Do not write to the curator asking him to send you photographs, maps or any other form of illustration – unless you are prepared to pay for them. Much the best thing is to ask him for a priced catalogue of any relevant material or illustrations which he can supply.

Very many sites are in the expert care of the Ministry of Public Building and Works, and guide-books to them, written by experts, are published by the Ministry at very low cost. *Sectional List No. 27 – Ancient Monuments and Historic Buildings,* obtainable from Her Majesty's Stationery Office and Government Bookshops, contains a list of them all. Another list, of all the picture postcards and colour slides of ancient monuments, can be obtained from The Clerk of Stationery, Ministry of Public Building and Works, Lambeth Bridge House, London, S.E.1.

It remains to add one very strong note of caution. The very act of excavation destroys much of the evidence; a vein of ash or coloured earth, a posthole, a coin or a stone cannot be accurately replaced once it has been dug up. Meticulous records have to be kept, and published as soon as possible. It is essential that no attempt at excavation be made unless under expert supervision, for the enthusiastic but inexperienced amateur can only do irreparable damage. Digging up history can be absorbing, but it must be done in the right way. How can the novice learn?

First, the school holidays provide ample time for ambitious projects, such as visiting and recording sites, tracing Roman roads, studying or helping in the local museum. Secondly, there are numerous opportunities offered on excavations where sympathetic directors are prepared to accept young people as volunteer helpers. Of course, not all excavation directors have the time or the facilities to look after young volunteers. Information of this kind about excavations, or training schools or courses, is to be found in the *Calendar of Excavations*.

Here is a list of books about Roman Britain. General works are placed first; an asterisk against a title indicates that the book is probably more suitable for non-specialist readers.

GENERAL WORKS

*A. BIRLEY, *Life in Roman Britain*. Batsford.
E. BIRLEY, *Roman Britain and the Roman Army*. Titus Wilson.
P. HUNTER BLAIR, *Roman Britain and Early England*. Nelson.
*A. R. BURN, *Agricola and Roman Britain*. EUP.
A. R. BURN, *The Romans in Britain*. Blackwell.
M. CHARLESWORTH, *The Lost Province*. Univ. of Wales Press
COLLINGWOOD & J. N. L. MYRES, *Roman Britain and the English Settlements*. OUP.
S. S. FRERE, *Britannia*. Routledge, Kegan Paul.
J. LIVERSIDGE, *Britain in the Roman Empire*. Routledge, Kegan Paul.
R. W. MOORE, *The Romans in Britain*. Methuen.
*I. A. RICHMOND, *Roman Britain*. Penguin Books.
*I. A. RICHMOND, *Roman Britain: 'Britain in Pictures' Series*.
A. L. F. RIVET, *Town and Country in Roman Britain*. Hutchinson.
*J. M. C. TOYNBEE, *Art in Roman Britain*. Phaidon.
*S. THOMAS, *Pre-Roman Britain*. Studio Vista.
LONGMAN HISTORY PROJECT KIT: *Roman Britain*

SEPARATE TOPICS

E. BIRLEY, *Research on Hadrian's Wall*. Titus Wilson.
*G. C. BOON, *Roman Silchester*. Max Parrish.
*BRITISH MUSEUM. *Guide to the Antiquities of Roman Britain*.
*J. COLLINGWOOD BRUCE & I. A. RICHMOND, *Handbook to the Roman Wall*.
R. G. COLLINGWOOD & R. P. WRIGHT, *The Roman Inscriptions of Britain*. OUP.
*L. COTTRELL, *The Great Invasion*. Pan Books.

*D. R. DUDLEY & G. WEBSTER, *The Rebellion of Boudicca*. Routledge, Kegan Paul.
*D. R. DUDLEY & G. WEBSTER, *The Roman Conquest of Britain*. Batsford.
*S. S. FRERE, *Roman Canterbury*. Canterbury Excav. Comm.
S. S. FRERE (Editor), *Problems of the Iron Age in Southern Britain*. Institute of Arch. London University.
M. R. HULL & C. F. HAWKES, *Camulodunum*. Society of Antiquaries.
M. R. HULL, *Roman Colchester*. Society of Antiquaries.
M. J. T. LEWIS, *Temples in Roman Britain*. CUP.
R. P. MACK, *The Coinage of Ancient Britain*. Spink.
*I. D. MARGARY, *Roman Roads in Britain*. Phoenix.
*I. D. MARGARY, *Roman Ways in the Weald*. Phoenix.
*G. W. MEATES, *Lullingstone Roman Villa*. Heinemann.
*G. W. MEATES, *Guide to Lullingstone Roman Villa*. HMSO.
R. MERRIFIELD, *The Roman City of London*. Benn.
S. N. MILLER, *Severus in Britain*. Cambridge Ancient History, vol. xii.
I. A. RICHMOND (Editor), *Roman and Native in North Britain*. Nelson.
A. L. F. RIVET (Editor), *The Roman Villa in Britain*. Routledge, Kegan Paul.
*A. S. ROBERTSON, *The Antonine Wall*. Glasgow Arch. Soc. Handbook.
*F. W. THOMPSON, *Deva: Roman Chester*. Grosvenor Museum, Chester.
J. S. WACHER (Editor), *Cantonal Capitals of Roman Britain*. Leicester Univ. Press.
*G. WEBSTER, *The Roman Army*. Grosvenor Museum, Chester.
R. E. M. WHEELER, *Maiden Castle*. Society of Antiquaries.

The articles in specialist journals, like *The Antiquaries Journal* or *Archaeologia Aeliana*, are too numerous to mention, though these are invaluable for the serious student. It would be unfair, however, not to mention the name of D. F. Allen. I ought not to lay the blame for this book on his shoulders, but it was his famous article on the coins of the Belgae in *Archaeologia XC* that first aroused my own interest in Roman Britain.

References

Here are the references to the passages from ancient authors which have been quoted in this book.

Chapter 1
CAESAR, *de Bello Gallico*, IV. 20, 21; V. 12–14.
HERODOTUS, Bk. III, *c.* 115. Writes in Greek.
STRABO, 1.4.2; 2.4.1; 4.5.2–4. Greek.
APPIAN, 14.4.5. Greek.
DIODORUS SICULUS, V. 22.2. Greek.

Chapter 2
CAESAR, *de B. G.*, V. 21; II. 4; II. 13.
SUETONIUS, *de vita Divi Juli*, *c.* 45.

Chapter 3
CAESAR, *de B. G.*, IV. 23; IV. 29, 31; V. 1.

Chapter 4
CAESAR, *de B. G.*, V. 2; 8 ff.; 19 ff.
BEDE, *Ecclesiastical History*, I. 2.
CICERO, *ad Att.*, iv. 18.

Chapter 5
DIODORUS SICULUS, I. 4.7. Greek.
DIO CASSIUS, 49.38.2; 53.22. Greek.
HORACE, *Odes*, I. 35; III. 5.
STRABO, 2.5.8; 4.5.3. Greek.
AUGUSTUS, *Res Gestae*, vi. 32.
SUETONIUS, *Caligula*, *c.* 44, 46.
TACITUS, *Agricola*, 13.

Chapter 6
JOSEPHUS, *Wars of the Jews III*, *c.* 72–105. Greek.

Chapter 7
SUETONIUS, *Claudius*, 17, 21.
DIO CASSIUS, 60. 19–22. Greek.
SUETONIUS, *Vespasian*, 4.
Anthologia Latina, 426.

Chapter 8
TACITUS, *Annals*, xii. 31–40.
ZONARAS, ii. 7. Greek.
TACITUS, *Agricola*, 14.

Chapter 9
TACITUS, *Annals*, xiv. 29–34, 36, 37.
DIO CASSIUS, 62.2. Greek.

Chapter 10
TACITUS, *Annals*, xiv. 38, 39. *Agricola*, 16, 17. *Histories*, I. 9, 60; III. 45.

Chapter 12
TACITUS, *Agricola*, 18–20, 22–24.

Chapter 13
TACITUS, *Agricola*, 25–30, 38.

Chapter 14
TACITUS, *Histories*, I. 2.
Historia Augusta, Hadrian, cc. 5, 11.
Pausanias, viii. 43. Greek.

Chapter 15
TACITUS, *Agricola*, 21.

Chapter 16
COLUMELLA, *de Re Rustica*, 1.48.
PLINY, *Natural History*, 34, 164.

Chapter 17
DIO CASSIUS, 72, 8. Greek.
Historia Augusta, Commodus, 6, 1–2.
Pertinax, 3. *Albinus*, 8–10, 13.
DIO CASSIUS, 76, 12–13, 15. Greek.

Chapter 18
Eutropius, ix, 21–22.
SIDONIUS APOLLINARIS, *Letters*, viii. 6, 14–15.
GIBBON, *Decline and Fall*, Vol. 1, Ch. 13.

Chapter 19
BEDE, *Ecclesiastical History*, I. 6.7.
SULPICIUS SEVERUS, *Sacred History*, ii. 41.

Chapter 20
TACITUS, *Agricola*, 11.

Chapter 21
AMMIANUS MARCELLINUS, xx. 1; xxvii. 8; xxviii. 3.

Chapter 22
PAULUS OROSIUS, vii. 34.9.
CLAUDIAN, *de Laudibus Stilichonis*, II. 247–255.
BEDE, *Ecclesiastical History*, I. 11.
ZOSIMUS, vi. 10. Greek.
PROCOPIUS, *de Bello Vandalico*, I. 2. Greek.

Here are the references to the inscriptions. Two are given for each inscription; the first is to the selection in *The Romans in Britain* by A. R. Burn, and the second to the collection in *Roman Inscriptions of Britain* by R. G. Collingwood and R. P. Wright.

	Burn	RIB
Chapter 7		
Cogidumnus	3	91
Triumphal Arch	1	—
Chapter 14		
Altar to Neptune	86	1319
Reinforcements	88	—
Verus' reinforcements	104	1322
Chapter 17		
Rebuilding by Senecio	168	1234

	Burn	RIB
Chapter 18		
Rebuilding by Constantius	190	1912
Carausius' milestone	189	2291, 2292
Chapter 19		
Nodens curse	58	306
Anociticus	160	1329
Serapis	181	658
Chapter 20		
Austalis	46	—

	Burn	RIB
Placida	40	295
Verecunda	49	—
Simplicia's coffin	72	690
Julia Materna	157	1182
Nectovelius	115	2142
Julius Valens	70	363
The boar hunt	136	1041
Wine jar	47	—
Oculist's stamp	66	—
Barathes	156	1171
Regina	159	1265
Rufus' letter		
British Museum Guide p.48		

Illustrations and Acknowledgments

We are grateful to the following for permission to reproduce photographs, maps and drawings.

1 Clay lamp. *Verulamium Museum and Photo Precision Ltd*
3 Spoon. *British Museum*
6 The Mildenhall Dish. *British Museum*

Chapter 1
8 The world according to Herodotus.
9 Model of an Iron-age chariot. *The National Museum of Wales*
10 Reconstruction of Little Woodbury. *Central Office of Information, Crown Copyright*
11 Primitive corn-grinding mill. *Mr Stanley Thomas*
11 Iron-age weaving equipment. *Mr Stanley Thomas*
11 Woven fragments. *Salisbury, South Wiltshire and Blackmore Museum*
13 Gaul and Britain
15 Caesar's Britain

Chapter 2
16 Stonehenge. *Cambridge University Collection, photograph by Dr. J. K. St Joseph*
17 Maiden Castle. *Ministry of Public Buildings and Works, Crown Copyright*
18 Roman Fort at Richborough. *Ministry of Public Buildings and Works, Crown Copyright*
19 Broch. *Aerofilms and Aero Pictorial Limited*
21 Skeleton, Maiden Castle, *Society of Antiquaries*
22 Iron-age invasions
23 Ploughshare and billhook. *Mr Stanley Thomas*
24 Celtic hand-mirror. *The Trustees of the British Museum*
25 Celtic ornamental shield. *The Trustees of the British Museum*
26 Torc. *The Trustees of the British Museum*
27 Leading tribes of Britain

Chapter 3
29 Plaque recording Caesar's arrival. *The author*
31 Invasion Route, 55BC
34 Roman warship. *Mansell Collection*

Chapter 4
36 July 7th, 54 BC
40 March to Cassivellaunus' fortress town at Wheathampstead
41 Ditch round Cassivellaunus' capital. *The author*

Chapter 5
43 Gold Stater and copies. *The Dickens Press*
45 Where the British tribes lived
46 Stater of Tincommius. *The Trustees of the British Museum*
46 Commius' stater. *The Trustees of the British Museum*
47 Atrebate horse. *Aerofilms and Aero Pictorial Limited*
48 Handle, Silchester. *His Grace the Duke of Wellington's Silchester Collection, Reading Museum*
49 Coin of Verica. *The Trustees of the British Museum*
49 Tasciovanus' Riconi stater. *The Trustees of the British Museum*
49 Vine on Verica's coins. *The Trustees of the British Museum*
49 Cunobelinus' ear of barley. *The Trustees of the British Museum*

Chapter 6
52 Tombstone of Optio. *Grosvenor Museum, Chester*
53 Tombstone of Marcus Favonius Facilis. *Colchester and Essex Museum*
55 Model of legionary soldier. *Grosvenor Museum, Chester*
56 Corner of the legionary fortress at Caerleon. *Aerofilms*
57 Plan of the Caerleon fortress. *National Museum of Wales*
57 Reconstruction of the corner. *National Museum of Wales*
59 Reconstruction of the Caerleon amphitheatre. *Nat. Mus. of Wales*
60 Auxiliary cavalryman. *City Museum, Gloucester*

Chapter 7
62 Inscription at Chichester. *Chichester Photographic Service Ltd*
64 Coin celebrating Claudius' triumph. *The Trustees of the British Museum*

65 Inscription from Claudius' triumphal arch. *Dr Graham Webster*
67 Skulls from war graves at Maiden Castle. *Society of Antiquaries*
67 Roman ballista bolt in Briton's spine. *Society of Antiquaries*
68 Fosse Way and Plautius' frontier zone

Chapter 8
71 The new area of operations
73 'Tortoise' from Trajan's Column. *Grosvenor Museum. Chester*
76 Cogidubnus' Palace at Fishbourne. *Thomson Newspapers Ltd*

Chapter 9
78 Model of Temple of Claudius at Colchester. *Colchester and Essex Museum*
79 Head of Claudius. *Colchester and Essex Museum*
82 Layer of burnt ash and clay at Verulamium. *Verulamium Excavation Committee and Prof S. S. Frere*
83 Boudicca group, Thames Embankment. *Keystone Press Agency*

Chapter 10
85 Classicianus' tombstone. *The Trustees of the British Museum*
88 Vespasian. *Mansell Collection*
89 Advance of Cerialis
90 Fortifications at Stanwick. *Society of Antiquaries*

Chapter 11
93 Roman roads
94 Typical Roman road
95 Leeming Lane. *Cambridge University Collection, photo by Dr. J. K. St. Joseph*
96 Road at Wheeldale Moor. *British Travel Association*
98 Groove in the road at Blackstone Edge. *Dr Ivan D. Margary*

Index

(Governors of Britain in capitals, Roman Emperors in italics)